DATE DUE

Demco No. 62-0549

You Are There

COMANCHE CAPTIVE

Bryce Milligan

You Are There

COMANCHE CAPTIVE

Bryce Milligan

★
TexasMonthlyPress

All illustrations by Charles Shaw

Texas Monthly Press
Post Office Box 1569
Austin, Texas 78767

A   B   C   D   E   F   G

Milligan, Bryce, 1953–
    Comanche captive / by Bryce Milligan ; illustrat-
ed by Charles Shaw.
        p.   cm.
    Summary: As the twelve-year-old daughter of
Texas pioneers, the reader makes decisions in or-
der to survive captivity by Comanches.
    ISBN 0-87719-157-3 : $3.95
    1. Comanche Indians—Captivities—Juvenile
fiction. 2. Indians of North America—Captivities—
Juvenile fiction. 3. Plot-your-own stories.
    4. Comanche Indians—Captivities—Fiction.
    5. Indians of North America—Captivities—Fiction.
    6. Plot-your-own stories.]
I. Shaw, Charles, 1941–   ill. II. Title.
P77.M63932Co   1990
[Fic]—dc20   90-30877
                                            CIP
                                            AC

I came to discover native America by a long and sometimes blundering path, which I began as a Boy Scout, making costumes and dancing (very badly indeed) at the Anadarko powwows in Oklahoma. I came to know several Native Americans later when they and I were minor league folksingers in the late sixties and early seventies. Finally, I have long read and admired the growing body of work by Native American poets and writers. To all the Cherokee, Cheyenne, Choctaw, Comanche, Creek, Dakota, Hopi, Kiowa, Klallam, and Navajo by whom I have been enlightened along the way, this little book is dedicated.

INTRODUCTION

It is the winter of 1870. You are Nancy O'Connell, the twelve-year-old daughter of pioneer parents who have established a home on the Frio River, some 75 miles west of San Antonio, Texas. You have a brother, Joey, who is nine, and a sister, Christina, who is six. A few days before Christmas, you and your brother will be captured by Comanches. By using common sense, you may be able to survive the experience. Bad judgement can be deadly. You may be able to escape, or you may choose not to escape. More often than one would think, captives of the Indians grew to think of themselves as Indians. You may find this the most interesting experience of all.

One basic fact you need to know for your initial choices is that the Comanches respect courage. A second fact you must recognize is that the world of the Comanches is vastly different from your own. To survive in this strange environment, and even to escape it, you must adapt to the ways of your captors. Like the real captives whose stories this book is based upon, most of your choices will depend upon what you learn during the captivity.

Summer in South Texas is hot, incredibly hot, but now that winter has arrived, you cannot tell which is worse, the sweating or the freezing. Father says it isn't one or the other, but the change itself. He might be right, you think, as you trudge up the frozen, snow-dusted hill. Only three days before, the sun had been warm enough to play outside with Joey and Christina, and you had worn the light-blue calico dress Mama made for you last Easter. But then the sky over the northern horizon had turned a deep blue beneath a low rolling bank of clouds. The blue norther had put an end to playing outside. First the wind shifted back and forth, tossing the trees and rattling down the last and highest of the pecans. Mama told you to pick them up before the storm arrived. It didn't take long—the dark wall of clouds rolled across the land with a frightening speed.

That night you ate the roasted and salted pecans, hot right out of the pan, as everyone huddled around the fireplace. Outside the wind didn't just howl, it roared. The sound was like that of a buffalo stampede: a rumbling, grumbling sort of thing that came as much from the ground as it did from the air. It was an exciting night in the little cabin beside the

Frio River. The family sang Christmas hymns, ate hot nuts, and worked on Christmas gifts. Almost none of the gifts would be surprises, since it is impossible to keep anything a secret in a one-room cabin. Still, somehow every year Father and Mama surprised you, Joey and Christina with something. Usually it was a pair of mittens or a scarf, which Mama knitted by firelight long after the children were in bed. But last year had been special. Father had gone into San Antonio — a nine-day trip, there and back — to buy winter supplies. That Christmas morning the children found their stockings full of apples! Father said that they must have come all the way down the Mississippi on a riverboat, across the Gulf to Galveston by ship, then in wagons to San Antonio. Even dented and bruised, they were delicious, and Mama made a pie you would remember as long as you lived. But the apples were not the only thing memorable about that Christmas. In San Antonio, Father had cut some cane and brought it home. Most of it he split into thin strips that Mama used later to weave chair bottoms and a sun shade for the cabin window. But on Christmas morning, you found that Father had done something else with the cane. There, decorated with

red cardinal feathers on one end, was a
flute. A real flute. Father had made it just
for you, carving a vine and leaves from
one end to the other. In the year since,
you had learned to play several of the
hymns and other tunes that Father whis-
tled so often. You remembered hearing
some of them sung a long time ago in a
big building with lots of people—but that
was before the family moved out to the
Frio.

This year you are making two cornhusk
dolls for Christina. She is six, just half
your age since you turned twelve in Oc-
tober, and she helped you choose which
cloth scraps to use for the dolls' dresses.
Joey is nine, and you and Mama are making him a case for the rifle Father hid
away in the rafters.

But just now you must gather kindling
wood for the fire. The storm winds broke
off many oak limbs, and the hill is littered
with them. One by one you drag them
down to the wood shed, where you break
up each limb into smaller pieces and pile
them in a corner where they will dry out
—and stay dry. Keeping a supply of dry
kindling is one of your main jobs during
the winter, along with keeping the rest of
the firewood covered and dry. Wet wood
makes a smoky fire, and smoke attracts
Indians.

The nearest neighbor is old man Guerra, who lives in a rock and adobe house about three miles downstream. Like your cabin, it has only one room, but you are impressed because it has real wooden floors. About five miles east of Señor Guerra's place, a little below the headwaters spring of the Sabinal River, lives the Johnson family—all seven of them, Mr. and Mrs. Johnson and their five boys. Other families are scattered here and there throughout the hills all the way back to San Antonio. To the west are a few prospectors, a settlement or two and some army posts along the trail to El Paso, a few ranches, and a lot of Indians.

Living so far out on the frontier, Indians are a constant worry, and Father's often-repeated warnings are a litany you have memorized: "In this part of the country, there are no friendly Indians.... If you see an Indian, don't stop running until you see me.... Don't ever go out of eyesight of the cabin alone...," and on and on. But the fact is, you have never actually seen an Indian. There were plenty of Comanches and Apaches in this part of the country during the Civil War, when all the Rangers and soldiers had gone off to fight in the East. But when the war was over, the first thing the state of Texas did was to organize a war to drive the Indians

—meaning the Comanches—away from the settled area of the state. Still, whenever settlers come together, they always tell new stories of a family murdered in their cabin or a child taken captive and never seen again. The Johnson boys all claimed to have seen a Comanche war band once. It made a funny story, since everyone said that the reason the warriors hadn't captured them was that even a Comanche could see that the boys would be more trouble than it was worth just to feed them.

"Nancy! Nancy!" Joey is calling you from down the hill. "Watch this!"

On a makeshift sled of split logs, Joey slides down the lower part of the trail, laughing as he tumbles into a small drift of snow. You begin dragging the last big limb down to join him. Father is chopping firewood with his big double-bit ax. It makes a ringing thud that echoes between the hills. A pale-white smoke rises from the cabin chimney, and the smell of venison sausage and biscuits reminds you that it is time to get out of the cold and eat lunch. "I'll stay inside this afternoon," you think, "and work on the dolls with Christina."

Joey, who is pulling his little sled up to meet you, stops in the path, a frozen look on his face. Suddenly time speeds up. Joey is screaming "Comanches!" and pulling at your coat. Father is rushing across the yard at you, the big ax raised high over his head. You hear Christina crying and see Mother appear in the cabin door, carrying a rifle in each hand. Her big skirts swirling, she drops one gun and raises the other to her shoulder. You see the puff of smoke a full second before you hear the blast. At the same time you hear a loud groan right behind you.

"How could I not hear them?" you wonder as you turn to see who it was that Mama shot. Not ten feet behind you, a Comanche sits astride a brown and white spotted pony, a startled look on his face. Strangely, time now seems to slow down, as you look curiously at this, the first Indian you have ever seen. On one of his arms is a small leather disc of some sort—a shield perhaps—in his other hand is a long lance, its sharp metal tip decorated with a dozen fluttering feathers. His face and chest are covered with red and yellow designs, muddy colors you think. Then you notice a small spot of bright red in the middle of his chest, which is growing larger. The expression of surprise still in his glassy eyes, the Comanche warrior slips sideways off the horse, collapsing in a heap directly in front of you. His lance, two feet taller than you are, falls across your shoulder.

Suddenly the pony snorts and rears, and all around you are Comanche warriors. Your father rushes by, yelling, "Run, Nancy! Run, Joey!" He buries his ax in the chest of another warrior, then yanks it free, splattering you and the snow with crimson. A horse knocks you to the ground. Its rider leans far out of the saddle and swoops up Joey, who is just standing there crying. You hear your mother's rifle sound again.

Do you run or stay and fight? If you decide to run back to the cabin, turn to page 35

If you decide to stay with your father and use the spear in your hands, turn to page 47

Your mind races. The decision has to be made immediately — before the brave with the torch reaches the cabin. Christina is safely in the cellar. Mama is dead. Father is dead. You are so angry and hurt that the idea of hiding while these savages burn down the cabin strikes you as something you just cannot do. You jam the rifle through the hole and fire. Load, cock, and fire. Load, cock, and fire. Glancing through the peephole you see that two are down. You keep firing. There is a pounding at the window. One of them is trying to break through the shutters. You try to yank the gun out of the firing hole. It's stuck! You pull again, wrenching at it. Just as it comes free, the shutters burst inward, and you see the point of an arrow gleam in the moonlight.

Life doesn't matter much at this point, so you drop the empty rifle and grab up one of the kitchen butcher knives. Rushing to the window, you scream all the bad words you ever heard as you slash at the warrior outside. But he is not frightened at all when he sees that his adversary is only a yellow-haired little girl. He laughs, pointing at the window and calling to his companions. Startled, you let down your guard for a moment. The cunning brave takes advantage of that one moment to

swiftly reach inside and grab your wrist. He wrenches away the knife and pulls you out through the window, throwing you roughly to the ground.

Another brave ties your hands together in front of you, then lifts you up and drops you onto the back of a little pinto pony. He mounts behind you and canters around the yard whooping while the others loot the cabin. "Stay in the cellar, Christina," you think. "Please keep her in the cellar, Lord."

The looting is over quickly. The raid has lasted too long, it seems, and the warriors are anxious to get away. Two of them quickly empty the little smokehouse of all its hanging meat, while two others tie the meat, the big iron skillet, some pans and other utensils onto three horses. Then suddenly they are all mounted and you are racing up the trail away from the cabin. In the moonlight you see where your father lies, face down, with a dozen arrows in him. Looking back, you see that the cabin is not in flames, and you thank God for keeping Christina out of the hands of these savages. As to your own fate, you have an idea from the stories you have heard that rather than kill you, they will try to keep you a captive, even try to turn you into a Comanche. You promise yourself that they will find you a lot more trouble than they expect.

As you ride through the night on trails you did not know existed, passing beyond all the familiar landmarks, it strikes you that there were no dead Comanches in front of the house. In all the gunfire, did they just drop to the ground? Did you wound any? Later, the little band stops for a bite to eat and a drink of water from a small creek. Dawn's light shows that most of the warriors do bear wounds, but none very serious. They must be used to it, you think, since almost all of them are covered with scars. Some of the older warriors' scars are outlined with zigzag tatoos.

Five warriors are in the band, one of whom seems very young, no more than fifteen or sixteen. Only a little taller than you are, this young Comanche seems interested in you. He talks to the older warrior who had ridden behind you during the night, pointing and gesturing. When you mount up again, he is sitting behind you.

As you ride, he tries to talk to you using a mixture of Comanche, broken Spanish, a few words of English, and lots of gestures. You get the idea that he is asking your name.

16

"Nancy," you finally say to him, pointing both thumbs at yourself. "Nancy O'Connell."

Turn to page 57

No one notices as you lead your horse away from the destroyed village. It is difficult to say why you are reluctant to leave Buffalo Tail and the others. They are certainly not friends, but they no longer seem like enemies either. As for the Rangers, you have heard them talked about all your life as protectors—and you thought of them that way yourself—but what they did to the village seems too cruel. You had imagined being rescued by them so often, but your imaginary rescue did not include anyone's dying. They just surrounded the village and said, "Give us the girl." How did it go so wrong? Maybe they thought the Comanches had already killed you, and so they punished the village. But all the children, and Joey. Why kill them? Couldn't they see that there were no warriors there? But regardless of what the Rangers did, you remind yourself that you are white, that you still have a sister who needs you, that your place is with her and not with a few miserable Comanches who do not even have a whole tepee among them.

The trail you pick up is obvious—some twenty iron-shod horses, running in a group, have trampled the grass flat in a line running due east. You urge your mount to a gallop and follow the trail as easily as if it were an open road. Just at dark, as you ride toward the gleam of a campfire, a rough voice stops you, "Whoa, Injun! Whar you think you're going?" The muzzle of a Colt revolver jabs you in the side as a big man pulls you right out of the saddle.

"Stop it!" you tell him. "I'm Nancy O'Connell, the girl you came to rescue."

"Well, shoot, honey," the Ranger says a little more gently. "We thought you was plumb dead."

Old man Guerra, who rode out with the Rangers, tells you about Christina. She is alive, but the experience left her shaken. "A little sick here, you know?" he says touching his forehead. Since she first appeared at Señor Guerra's door, Christina has not uttered a word. He describes how, all the way back to San Antonio, she remained silent as a stone. He got the basic facts of your capture from her only by asking questions and by interpreting her nods and odd looks. Señor Guerra left Christina with the family of Doc McAllen. You remember Mama talking about the McAllens and their six daughters. They were friends of your parents before you moved out to the Frio.

Over a meal of beans, biscuits, and black coffee, you tell the story of your capture by the Comanches and of living with them for ten weeks. "Has it only

been ten weeks?" you wonder to yourself. It seems like a whole lifetime since
you were making dolls with Christina
and singing carols, waiting for Christmas to come to the little cabin on the
Frio.

When the Rangers learn from you that
only five warriors are in the Comanche
camp, one of them an old medicine man,
they begin making plans to attack the village a second time.

"I'm right sorry that your little brother
got kilt in the action, Miss," a tall, slender
man says, his chest crisscrossed with am-
munition belts. "But they was arrows
flyin' ever which way, and we jest wasn't
looking for a kid dressed up like a
Comanche."

A big man with a curly gray beard says
to you, "It just happens like that. But
we've got to shoot the little ones too, you
know, or else they just grow up to go
around killing more white folks."

He is wearing a huge Bowie knife
strapped to his leg. You wonder if he was
the one who scalped Shaggy Bull. You
also wonder who was shooting arrows
"ever which way" besides Shaggy Bull.
Unless it was the boys. You shiver at the
thought of Joey and his two friends pro-
tecting the village with their tiny bows.
You bed down for the night in a wool

blanket, which is neither as warm nor as soft as a buffalo robe in a cozy tepee. It is hard to get to sleep. Will they really go back tomorrow and kill *everyone* else in the village? You see Spring Flower in your mind and imagine the big Ranger shooting her down—so she will never bear a Comanche baby. There is still time, you think. If you sneak out of camp now, you can get away and warn them. If you do that, though, there will be no turning back. You will never see Christina again. She is being well taken care of, you know that, but she needs you more now than ever. Or does she need you? You who have eaten the raw buffalo liver and liked it? You who have slept beside the murderers of your parents and not risen up to avenge the slaughter? The questions roll around in your mind until the darkest hour of the night between sunset and moonrise. You can see that the guard nearest the horses is dozing. Now is the time. You must decide.

If you decide to return to San Antonio and Christina, turn to page 129

If you decide to rejoin the Comanches, turn to page 55

As it turns out, even Comanches have the good sense not to adopt a child into the family of the man who killed the child's father, so Shaggy Bull gets your father's bay mare instead of you or Joey. Buffalo Tail is enthralled by the flute, it appears, so he adopts you into his lodge. Buffalo Tail and Bee Woman have a daughter, slightly older than you, named Spring Flower. He also has a second wife, Coyote Eyes, a strange woman who speaks very little. You wonder about her name, as she has the same black eyes as everyone else.

The five of you will live together in the central tepee. The first thing that happens the next morning is that Bee Woman and Spring Flower cut your long hair off to barely below your ears. All Comanche women wear their hair this way, but the men grow theirs long, braiding it and wrapping the braids with strips of fur. Your calico dress is replaced by a loose buckskin dress—with nothing underneath. In fact, the women seem to think the very idea of undergarments quite funny.

Joey too is given a buckskin shirt, though he is allowed to keep his denim pants and boots. But he is not so lucky as you are when it comes to the lodge he must live in. Buffalo Tail gives Joey to a poor woman, Little Smile, whose husband and two oldest sons had died four winters before.

That winter is called the Winter of Grief when anyone mentions it. Though the Comanches do not know the name of the disease, they describe an epidemic of cholera which wiped out more than half of the band in a single winter. Along one of the wagon trails leading west to Santa Fe but many days north of the present camp, the band had just finished a buffalo hunt when some women found a pile of *tahbay-boh* (white man) clothing and blankets beside some freshly dug graves. Of course, the women brought the things back to camp. Dancing Moon, the band's *puhakut* (or medicine man), immediately said he felt that the things meant bad medicine for the band. No one, not even the *tahbay-boh,* would leave such good blankets behind unless they were very bad magic.

Dancing Moon's predictions had not been accurate that year, so there was some argument about the blankets and clothing. In the end, however, the Indians left the blankets and clothing behind when they moved south. But this time, Dancing Moon's medicine was strong, and his fears proved true: People began to get sick and die within a couple of weeks. More than forty members of the band died that winter, and only two babies had been born healthy since. Now the band stays far south of the wagon trail, even though that means they are now almost entirely cut off from the big northern buffalo herds.

Life in the winter camp goes in fits and starts. There is plenty of daily work for you to do—mainly gathering firewood and antelope chips for fuel. Then you learn to look for the roots of the sego lilies along the stream and other edible roots like wild onions and radishes. Soon, however, Bee Woman, Spring Flower, and even Coyote Eyes begin to teach you other things: how to sew and mend tepee skins and leather clothing and how to butcher and cook the fresh kills that are almost the sole food source for the tribe. Unless meat cannot be had, plants are used only for seasoning.

The large buffalo herds no longer come this far south on the plains, leaving the fast pronghorn antelope as the next largest food source. The adult hunters spend their days trying to drive these animals close to Dancing Moon, who holds two magic antelope hooves over his head.

When the antelope get close to the *puhakut,* the women, children, and old men make a large circle into which the warriors on horseback drive the antelope. Once in the circle, everyone begins shouting at the animals, which leap back and forth in confusion. Finally everyone rushes in with knives and clubs.

It seems a brutal way to hunt and not very efficient, since most of the antelope escape once the rush is made. Nor do you understand Dancing Moon's role in the process. Sometimes, of course, the hunters fail to drive any antelope to Dancing Moon. At other times, a hunter may come in with a single carcass across his horse. Often that antelope must feed the whole band for a day, and one antelope does not go very far. You, who have always had more than enough to eat, feel constantly hungry. Hunger does not seem to bother the Comanche adults or children very much—they eat when there is something to eat. Although coyotes are plentiful, the Comanches will not eat them. Nor will they eat birds or fish. Throughout the winter, it is red meat or nothing, with none of the kill being wasted. One reason you feel hungry all of the time is that when game is brought down, much of it is eaten raw, including much of the innards.

The Comanches think you and Joey are very picky.

The boys Joey's age and younger spend their days hunting small game, rabbits mainly, along with an occasional badger. Joey must learn quickly how to use the short Comanche bow, because he is expected to help feed his adopted family. Little Smile has a daughter, around seven years old, and the two of them have been living on the roots, nuts, and berries Little Smile gathered during the fall. They get meat only when another lodge has some to spare. Thus, if Joey wants to eat, he must learn to hunt. You watch him sometimes, running with the other boys or doing chores around the camp. His hair, which was brown to begin with, is now visibly darker from not washing. He seems to enjoy the hunting, has learned to shout a few words of Comanche when playing games with the other boys, and is just as dirty as any of them. Except for his denim pants, you think, it would be hard to tell him from the others.

As small as this camp is, you still do not see much of Joey. The antelope circle hunt brings you together at last for a few whispered words. You know that the confusion of the kill will last only half an hour or so, but you decide to ask Joey if he thinks you can escape.

"Do you know how to get home?" he asks.

"There's no home to go back to," you say. "But we came west and then north. If we just head east, maybe we'll cross a wagon trail we can follow. Or we can just keep going until we get to Austin."

"I don't know," says Joey. "It is awfully cold to be away from a tepee and a fire."

"Joey, we don't belong in a tepee. We belong in a house where they have warm beds and where they cook food properly."

"I guess you're right, Singing . . . I mean, Nancy. If you think we can make it, I'll go with you."

The decision is yours. Buffalo Tail has said more than once that the band ought to move north to Yellow Creek where there might be more game. That will only make escape more difficult and the road back longer. The sky is clear now, but it is still winter, and you know that a norther could blow in at any time. Crossing the high plains with the Comanches after you will mean not making a fire for several days, hiding in the grass like coyotes, with only pemmican to eat. You won't be able to steal a horse, but you can probably sneak back to camp for a robe and some pemmican before you make a run for it. On the other hand, it has been only six or

30

seven weeks since your capture. Have old man Guerra and the Rangers had time to track you down? Should you wait on them any longer? Can they find you even if they did come this far onto the plains?

Do you try to escape, or do you stay?
If you decide to escape, turn to page 97

If you decide to stay, go on to next page.

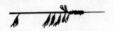

Escape, you finally decide, must wait for warmer weather. There is no reason to risk being recaptured and almost certainly killed, just to end up freezing to death.

It is near the end of February when Shaggy Bull and Hiding Rabbit ride into camp and announce that they have sighted two stray buffalo bulls. Late winter is known among the Comanches as the Moon of Babies Crying for Food, so this is good news indeed. The mood of the village changes immediately from one of quiet patience to joyful anticipation. The warriors start at once to paint themselves for the hunt. The women, children (Joey among them), and old people begin gathering firewood for the feast and building drying racks to preserve the meat. If the buffalo were farther away or if a whole herd were near, the village would simply move to the site of the hunt. Since there are only two bulls and they are close by, the meat and skins will be packed back to the village after the buffalo are butchered.

Spring Flower, Coyote Eyes, Bee Woman, and you prepare to ride with the hunters. You are going to learn how to butcher a buffalo. The hunters include Buffalo Tail, Hiding Rabbit, He Who Spits, and

Morning Wind. Dancing Moon accompanies you not to join the hunt but to make the proper magic. Shaggy Bull is remaining as guardian of the camp—a role with some honor to it, though the warrior visibly longs to join the hunt.

The buffalo are three hours north of the camp. The February cold is bitter, but still, it is a relief to get out of the camp and be doing something.

Turn to page 67

Hiding Rabbit has a firm grasp of the bridle. Before you know it he has pulled you off the rearing horse and thrown you to the ground. Your head strikes a rock, and immediately you lose consciousness. The last thing you see is Hiding Rabbit drawing his knife. Then you know no more.

End

Your mother is screaming for you to all run to the cabin. At the same time she is firing and reloading the big buffalo gun as fast as she can. She had killed the first Indian with the old flintlock squirrel rifle—Joey's Christmas present. It was an accurate rifle, but slow to load. Mama managed to get off a couple of shots a minute with Father's bigger and newer but less accurate Sharps Carbine. Father used to tease Mama when he'd tell her, "If the Comanches attack, just keep shooting —you may not hit any, but you'll come close to scaring them to death." That was exactly what she was doing, but it was no longer funny.

As you reach the cabin door, Mama yells for you to keep Christina inside, so you quickly go in and push your little sister under you parents' bed. You pull the window shutters to and lock them. All you can find for a weapon is Mama's big butcher knife. You pick it up and stand by the door as you hear an arrow thud against it.

Only now that you have time to think do you begin to feel truly frightened. You are so scared that you want to vomit, and you have to hold onto the wall to keep from fainting. Then you hear Mama scream. You yank the door open. Mama

stumbles through.

"Lock it!" she says, and you struggle to get the big crosspiece into place. You can feel the impact of a Comanche lance against the door.

Then you turn to help Mama. An arrow, broken off a few inches from the tip by her fall, protrudes from her shoulder. Another, a little more than two feet long, has transfixed her calf.

"Father?" you ask her.

"Dead," she says. "And they got away with little Joey."

She motions for you to take the gun, so you pick it up and walk to the table where the big .50 caliber cartridges lay scattered. You insert a cartridge and put the heavy gun to one of the peepholes Father had left in the mud chinking between the logs. Peering outside, you see three Comanche braves, prancing about on their ponies in front of the house. One is waving something over his head and shouting words you cannot understand. But then you know what he is waving. The mass of black hair is your father's scalp. You pull the trigger.

Turn to page 79

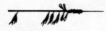

You decide to keep your promise to Mama. As quietly as possible, you tip-toe to the cellar. You are just about to crawl in when you realize that you must leave the gun in the cabin—the Comanches will miss it and then realize that you are hiding. Quickly you put the gun down beside Mama, and kiss her on the cheek. You've heard the stories about what Comanches do to captive white women, and you realize that she is far better off dead than alive—she always said she would rather die than be captured—but still your eyes are swimming with tears as you look at her cold, crumpled form on the floor. Only fear and your promise to Mama can tear you away from her body. Slowly you retreat on your hands and knees across the floor to the cellar hole. Once inside, you pull the covering boards over the hole.

The little cellar is just barely big enough to hold both you and Christina, but you squeeze in and hug Christina, who is shivering with fear and cold. It is not long before you hear the crackle of flames. The log walls burn rapidly and soon begin to collapse. The rafters crack and crash to the ground, followed by the big ridgepole and the rest of the roof. The boards above you begin to grow very hot, and you wish that you had thought to douse them with water before you covered the hole. Soon the chill of the cold earth gives way to a stifling heat. Fortunately very little smoke settles in the hole. Still, breathing becomes more and more difficult. It is all you can do to keep from coughing and gasping out loud for breath, so you concentrate on taking slow, even, quiet breaths. You time your breathing to a short prayer you keep repeating in your mind. "Joey," you pray, "please don't let them torture little Joey, not little Joey, Lord, please." Christina, you are thankful, seems to have passed out.

Although it seems forever, it is all over in a few hours. You can hear the Comanches poking through the ruins over your head. They work quickly since they know that such a fire will attract the attention of any settlers in the area. Almost everything is completely burned up, but the Comanches still break up what is left of the table, the bed frame, even Mama's beautiful cane-bottom chairs. The feather mattress that Mama prized so much—a smoldering mess—is hacked to pieces amid frenzied laughter, and feather bits and down scatter like snow on the ruined cabin. Finally the Indians ride off, taking only the big iron skillet, a few knives, pots and pans, and other metal utensils. Apparently they never even thought to look for you.

You do not dare to get out of the cellar yet, but pushing aside the charred boards over your heads, you can at least breathe now. The warmth generated by the cabin fire is long gone by morning. Still, you wait until the sun is high overhead before you dare to venture out. Cold, cramped, and weary, you wriggle out of the hole. Everything you knew in the world yesterday is gone now. Amid the ruins of the cabin you called home, only the stone chimney is left standing. Across the yard, Father lies where he fell, pierced by a dozen arrows. Mama—you hardly dare look—Mama's body is badly burned and, even worse, mutilated.

The sun is clear and bright on a cold December afternoon in the Hill Country of South Texas, shedding its light on a scene of utter and complete desolation.

"Come on," you tell Christina. "Let's bury them before we leave here."

Silent, as she will be the rest of her life, Christina begins gathering the stones that will mark your parents' graves. The frozen ground is hard and unyielding to your shovel, but eventually the job is done. You make Christina turn away while you bring what the Comanches and the fire left of your mother. It makes you physically ill, and you are forced to retch more than once before you manage to get Father and Mama together in the single grave. You pile stones on the graves to keep away the wild animals, and Christina marks the site with a cross of cedar wood.

Weeping and holding hands, you head south along the stream.

End

Since it is common knowledge that Comanches despise cowards, you see no need to even try to reason with them. Hanging on to the mane of the little pony, you kick it as hard as you can. Rearing briefly, it knocks down Hiding Rabbit and then takes off at a dead run back up the trail. An arrow whistles by you — Hiding Rabbit is *really* mad — then there is a lot of shouting on the trail behind you.

Your freedom is short-lived. Within a minute or so, another brave races up beside you and leans over to take the reins out of your hands.

"No good escape, girl," he says.

You are shocked to hear English, and you look at the warrior who has now stopped both horses. He is an older man, and a few streaks of gray show in his otherwise jet-black hair. Leading the horses back to the group gathered around Hiding Rabbit on the trail, he speaks again to you.

"Call me Buffalo Tail. You?"

"Nancy O'Connell," you say.

"What 'Nancy' mean?" he asks you.

"Nothing," you reply. "It is just a name — what my parents called me when I was born." You feel confused talking so calmly to this murderer about your name and your parents.

"Brave girl need better name," he says. He talks to the band for a few minutes in Comanche, during which the mood eases and Hiding Rabbit half smiles. Turning back to you, Buffalo Tail says, "I tell them, girl fight like hurt bull. Make good Comanche. You ride with Hiding Rabbit, you stay alive. Run off again, he kill you. We join others soon."

You think for a while. There is nothing particularly *kind* in what Buffalo Tail said to you, but it is clear that they would rather have you alive. And who are the others? Is Joey with them? You'll have a better chance of escaping with Joey than alone—and besides, you can't leave Joey alone among the Indians either. You decide that you will have to put up with Hiding Rabbit, no matter what he tries to do to you.

Once he is mounted behind you again, you find out immediately what your punishment is for embarrassing him. He rips your dress off your shoulders and down to your hips, leaving you as embarrassed as he was. But you find out quickly that the punishment is not that you have to be half-naked in front of all these men—they don't seem to notice—but that you may well freeze to death. Only after another hour's ride, when you begin to sneeze, does Hiding Rabbit pull up the dress for you. Buffalo Tail gives you a smelly fur to wrap up in. This buffalo robe is the first item of Comanche clothing you must wear. As thankful as you are for its warmth, you hope it will be the last.

At sundown, your band reaches the crest of a hill crowned with oak trees. To the west stretches a broad flat expanse of grasslands. You have entered Comancheria, from which few whites have ever returned. Waiting on the hill is another small band of Comanches. They have with them the bodies of the warriors killed by your father's ax and Mama's first rifle shot. They also have Joey. You rush over to him, but he cannot get up to meet you. He has been beaten badly, and there are bruises showing all around his head and shoulders. He has a knife wound as well, a long gash running from shoulder to elbow on his right arm. You kneel down next to him.

"What happened at home?" Joey asks.

"I think Christina's alive," you whisper.

"Mama? And Father?"

"Dead," you say.

"Oh, Nancy," he moans. "Did they do anything . . . terrible to them?"

"I don't know if they did anything bad to Mama—I'm almost certain she was dead by the time they got into the cabin. But they scalped Father." Looking over at the two bodies draped across the horses standing nearby, you add, "Mama shot that one, and Father got the other one with his ax."

"Yeah, I saw that before they rode off with me. I sure was worried about you and Chris. I'm glad you're alright."

Can you use that arm?" you ask.

"Yeah, but it hurts. Bad."

"Tried to get away, didn't you?"

Joey smiled a little. "I showed them I wouldn't go easy."

"Me too," you say and settle down beside him to exchange stories—and weep—and wait to see what will happen next.

Turn to page 61

Grabbing up the long lance, you jab it at the nearest Comanche, turning him away from Father. The point of the lance is a wickedly sharp piece of jagged iron. You slash at the warrior with it, cutting him across his thigh. Rather than howl with pain, however, he seems almost amused. Shouting something to his companions, he points at you and laughs. That infuriates you and you jab at him again, this time taking a piece of flesh out of his arm. Without any laughter, he slaps the spear away from you and shoves you roughly to the ground. Father makes a lunge for him, but you are horrified to see Father fall, pierced by several arrows. One of the mounted archers leaps to the ground next to Father, tapping him on the head with his bow and crying "*Aaa-hey!*" Another warrior does so as well. Then, before your horrified eyes, the first one pulls out a big hunting knife and circles Father's head, yanking free his hair and scalp with a sickening pop. Dancing and waving the bloody scalp, he infuriates you. You are up and rushing at him before you know it, but a big arm reaches out and stops you. There is nothing left to fight with, so you bite him as hard as you can. He slaps you to the ground, then deftly ties your hands in front of you with a

rawhide thong. Just as quickly, he throws you up onto a pinto pony as he mounts behind you. He canters about the yard whooping, daring your mother to shoot at him. She doesn't, for fear of hitting you.

From the door of the cabin, Mama fires away at the other Comanches with the big rifle, and you can see little Christina beside her, hidden in Mama's big calico skirts, handing her cartridges. You hope the warriors do not notice Christina. But then you see two braves approaching Mama from the sides of the house. You try to call out a warning, but it is too late. As you watch horrified, an arrow pierces Mama's calf. Turning toward the house, she receives another in the shoulder. The door slams shut.

The rest of the day the Comanches periodically run toward the house with a torch, only to be forced back by Mama's rifle fire. Toward dark, however, the sound of the rifle ceases, meaning, you are sure, that Mama is dead. The warriors quickly break into the cabin through the one window. Its locked shutters fall inward after only a couple of thrusts with a log. You pray that Christina remembers the plan for such a situation. The cabin floor is dirt except for a few boards covering a small root cellar. The children were to hide in the tiny space if Indians attacked. That way, if the cabin burned down, whoever was in the root cellar would survive the fire. You don't hear Christina's voice as the warriors crawl in and out of the window, loading up their horses with Mama's big iron skillet, pans, and other kitchen utensils. They break into the little smokehouse behind the cabin, carry out all the hanging meat in it, and strap that too across the horses.

Without any further delays, the little band mounts up and rides into the night, up the very trail where you had gathered kindling this morning. It seems so long ago. You pass the place where your father lies, face down, with a dozen arrows in him. Looking back, you see that the cabin is in flames, and you pray that Christina will stay safe in the cellar. Still, you are thankful that Christina is not in the hands of these savages. As to your own fate, you have an idea from the stories you have heard that rather than kill you, they will try to keep you captive, even try to turn you into a Comanche. You promise yourself that they will find you a lot more trouble than they expect. Soon, however, your anger gives in to grief, and you weep as you never have before. Mama and Father lie dead in the night, Christina is surely frightened out of her wits, and Joey is a captive, like you. Or could he have escaped? Or is he dead?

As you ride through the night on trails you did not know existed, passing beyond all the familiar landmarks, it occurs to you that there were no dead Comanches in front of the house. In all the gunfire, did they just drop to the ground? Were any even wounded? Later, the little band stops for a bite to eat and a drink of water from a small creek. Dawn's light shows that most of the warriors do bear wounds, though none are very serious. They must be used to it, you think, since almost all of them are covered in scars. Some of the older warriors have zigzag tatoos outlining their biggest scars. Five warriors are in the band, one of whom seems very young, no more than fifteen or sixteen. Only a little taller than you are, this young Comanche seems interested in you. He talks to the older warrior who had ridden behind you during the night, pointing and gesturing. When you mount up again, he is sitting behind you.

As you ride, he tries to talk to you. Using a mixture of Comanche, broken Spanish, a few words of English, and lots of gestures, you get the idea that he is asking your name.

"Nancy," you finally say to him, pointing both thumbs at yourself. "Nancy O'Connell."

Turn to page 57

There is nothing you can do for Christina, you decide, that is not being done for her by the McAllens. Doc McAllen, his wife, and their six daughters will surely take good care of her. You would only be an oddity—the girl who lived with the Comanches. On the other hand, you really can help Buffalo Tail. You can save what is left of the band from being slaughtered.

Your pony is tethered with the rest of the remuda. You walk quietly past the slumbering guard, who lies shivering on his blanket. Two other guards are still awake, talking by the fire. The horses are about thirty yards away from the fire. You lead your pony away, fifty, then a hundred yards. All is quiet.

"If I am going to join the Comanches," you think, "I'd better start thinking like one." You tether your pony to a dead branch lying on the ground. One by one, you lead a dozen horses away from the Ranger camp. Finally, you cut off a lock of your yellow hair and tie it onto the rope to which the horses were tethered. Maybe that will tell them something. Linking the reins from one horse to another, you walk them silently into the night. When you are a good mile away, you break into a canter that lasts until you arrive at Buffalo Tail's now deserted camp. With a last lingering look at the dark bundles cradled in the leafless arms of the trees along the creek—halfway between earth and sky—you head north.

Just before sunrise, you come upon Buffalo Tail's new camp. They too have traveled most of the night, burdened down by the buffalo meat from yesterday's hunt and the few tepee poles and other items salvaged from the old camp. You tie the horses beside the hastily constructed lodge where the exhausted remnant of the band is sleeping. You sit down and wait for the dawn.

Turn to page 147

"Nancy," he repeats slowly. Pointing to himself, he says a long word that you cannot repeat. Later you will find that it means something like "Hiding Rabbit," but for now, you just turn forward again. You are *not* going to carry on a polite conversation with this murderer, you tell yourself. You sit up stiff and straight, not turning at all when he continues to talk.

Pretty soon you feel his hands in your hair. You've heard that Indians are fascinated by blond hair, so you let this go on as long as you can stand it, then toss your head to show that you don't like it. Hiding Rabbit thinks this is funny and goes right on pulling at it, twining his fingers in it, now and then actually pulling a strand out. Finally you cannot stand it anymore and hit him violently in the ribs with your elbow. He responds by slapping you on the side of the head, making your ears ring. Then he does something far worse. He tears loose the buttons down the back of your dress and puts his hands inside.

You throw all your weight backward against Hiding Rabbit's chest, knocking him right off the back of the pony. This is a terrible insult to him, you realize at

once, since the whole band is now laughing at him. He rises with an angry look, grabbing hold of the horse's bridle.

Do you try to ride down Hiding Rabbit and escape? If you try to escape, turn to page 43

If you decide to wait it out, turn to page 33

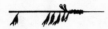

The two dead warriors are buried— with very little ceremony—by placing their bodies and weapons in a small cave. Turning from the hill, the band heads west. The next few days are spent riding and camping, riding and camping, until you lose track of the days and the land- marks. Actually very few landmarks are to be seen—the hills quickly disappeared behind you, and now you are riding through a vast ocean of grass. It is often as tall as the shoulders of the horses, and you realize that there will be no way for you to retrace the path back home, even if you do escape. Behind you, there is only a vague line visible through the grass where the band has passed, and once the wind has stirred the grass even a little, that too vanishes.

You try counting the days since you were captured, but they seem as feature- less as the grass, even though it can only have been nine or ten days in all. You promise yourself that you will try very hard to keep better track of the days, and you make Joey promise as well.

Trying to count the days, however, brings you to the conclusion that this, to- day, must be Christmas Day or the day af- ter. You try to recite the Christmas story from the second chapter of Luke. Father had been helping you and Joey memorize it just before the attack. It is comforting in a way to think that Mary and Joseph were in a worse fix than you are now. There was a king trying to kill the Baby Jesus, and they had to cross a desert to go to Egypt. Looking around you, at the desolate plains, you think, "It could be worse. This could be a real desert." Mama always had everyone count their blessings at Christmas dinner. Let's see. Joey's arm is healing. Christina is alive. None of the family was tortured. But the blessings pale beside the fact that Mama and Father are dead, murdered by these men around you.

How can they imagine that you will "make a good Comanche" when the sight of them can only remind you of Mama and Father riddled with arrows? Shaggy Bull, one of the band's forward scouts, has sighted the village and is whooping from the hill ahead. You know that your father's hair dangles even now from his shield. You'll kill him, you promise yourself. You'll find a way somehow, someday.

But despite your anger, you think, you will be happy to get off this horse and sleep under a roof—even if that roof is a Comanche tepee. Your inner thighs are rubbed raw from the stiff buffalo hide saddle, and your wrists, still tied together, are a mess of scabs. Not being able to stretch out your arms, together with the cold, has given your shoulders endless muscle cramps. Yes, you will be glad to get off this horse.

The village is still an hour's ride ahead, and you spend the time talking to Joey about what to expect. This far into their own territory, the Comanches have no fear that you will try to escape, so they have allowed you one horse each, though your hands are still tied.

"Do you think they'll kill us?" asks Joey.

"No," you reply. "They've taken too much trouble to keep us alive. They'll either keep us as slaves or maybe try to trade us to the Mexicans for supplies. In any case, Father told me once that captives belong to the families of any men who are killed on a raid."

"I wouldn't think they would want us, do you?"

"I don't know," you say. "They think about these things differently than we do." You do not tell him about your promise of vengeance on Shaggy Bull. Nor do you tell him the other reason the band has for keeping you alive. Buffalo Tail said that the Pehnahterkuhs need strong women to bear more babies for the tribe. That did not bother you too much at first, since you are only twelve. But it has since occurred to you that your age does not seem to bother Hiding Rabbit very much. Since his initial embarrassment, he has been watching you with a strange look. The touching continued too, while you had to ride double with him, but you've just had to accept it. You are not sure whether that has to do with Hiding Rabbit being a Comanche or not. After all, Johnny Johnson tried to do something similar to you last summer. Johnny, however, had not ripped your dress off when you screamed. Johnny had taken off like a scared rabbit.

Of course, everyone in Texas knew the story of Cynthia Ann Parker. Father told the sad sad story several times to you and Joey. Cynthia was nine years old when the Comanches had captured her, and by the time she was fifteen, she was married to Chief Nocona and she was the mother of Quanah. Her son was supposed to be the smartest and meanest Comanche war chief ever. When Cynthia was finally recaptured by some soldiers, they say she was more Comanche than white. You think a lot about Cynthia Ann as you ride across the plains.

With your parents dead, there is no telling how long it will take Christina to get to old man Guerra's place. Then he would have to ride back to San Antonio to get a posse of Rangers to come after you. That will take several days, and the trail will be cold, impossible to follow even for Rangers.

"I have to realize that no one is going to save us," you tell yourself. "I live in a different world now, with different rules. I'll have to learn them or die."

On the other hand, you promise yourself, the first real chance you have to escape with Joey, you'll take it. In the meantime, you must make certain that you do not lose count of the days and that you do not ever forget who you really are. You will *not* be like Cynthia Ann, you tell yourself. Over and over, you recite in your mind: "I am Nancy O'Connell. I am not a Comanche. My mother and father were Sarah and Joseph Edward O'Connell. We lived on the Frio River. I was born on May 1, 1858. I am Nancy O'Connell. I am not a Comanche...."

Turn to page 83

Hiding Rabbit rides ahead to see whether the buffalo have moved overnight. The women lag behind the warriors, chatting about this and that while you try to understand their strange language. Already you have picked up a number of words, but when you try to put them together in a sentence, the women always laugh.

Buffalo Tail does not laugh, since he knows how hard it was for him to learn English. Instead, he just corrects your mistakes. In turn, he expects you to help him learn new words in English. Buffalo Tail learned English, he told you when you asked him about it—from another captive, a white boy about his own age who had died years ago fighting the Lipan Apaches. The two had grown up and become warriors together, then on a raid into Mexico they had run into the Apaches. That was the whole story as Buffalo Tail told it.

You have learned a lot about the Comanches talking to Buffalo Tail across the fire in the tepee at night. For one thing, they do not call themselves Comanches, but Nermernuh, which simply means "People." And they are not really one big tribe, but several large groups, like the Pehnahterkuhs, the

"Honey Eaters" or "Wasps." The groups consist of many small bands, some of which are really just extended families that camp together. The Pehnahterkuhs were once the largest of the Comanche groups, holding most of the Hill Country and western plains of southern Texas. Buffalo Tail's is one of the last Pehnahterkuh bands still free. The rest have been killed or have gone to the reservation lands north of the Red River.

North of the Pehnahterkuh are the lands of the Nokoni ("Those Who Turn Back"), then the Kotsoteka ("Buffalo Eaters"), the Kwerhar-rehnuh ("Antelopes"), whose young war chief was the famous Quanah Parker, the son of Cynthia Ann, and finally far to the north, the Yampah-reekuh ("Yap-root Eaters"). Related in some way, but not truly of the Nermer-nuh, were the Kiowas, a tribe that roamed some of the same country as the Buffalo Eaters and Antelopes.

The Comanches do not have any allies, but they do have plenty of enemies, chief among them the Lipan Apaches to the south and the Tonkawas. You have always heard that the Tonkawas were friendly Indians, scouting for the Rangers and the army against the Comanches. What is confusing is that the reason the Comanches hate the Tonkawas is not just that they help the Whites but also that they are cannibals! Buffalo Tail cannot begin to describe his loathing for that practice.

Trying to put all this together, keeping the names and stories straight, occupies you when you can no longer follow the conversation of Spring Flower and the other women. As poor as this band is, you can tell from the way Buffalo Tail talks about the Nermernuh that they are a proud people. Once they were the most powerful people in their world—a world that is changing rapidly. They know what metal is, for example, but have no idea how it is made. Buffalo Tail thinks about this a lot, he says. Sometimes he will just stare at a copper kettle or a black iron skillet or the intricate works of a gun and ask you to explain how these things are made. You can tell him only what you heard your father say about it once— about mining and melting down metal out of rocks—but it makes little sense to the chief.

When Hiding Rabbit reappears, he tells of yet another mystery. The buffalo, he says, are acting strange, a little crazy, and there is a terrible scent in the air. The group rides forward to investigate. Over a small rise, you sight two large buffalo bulls. The buffalo mill about, not as if they are looking for grass but as if they are lost in some way. You wonder how they became separated from their herd.

Puzzling out this mystery will have to wait. The hunters strip down to breech-clouts and moccasin-boots, then mount and ride away upwind of the animals. Dancing Moon chants, his arms outstretched, facing the east. Suddenly the braves are racing down on the buffalo, Hiding Rabbit and Morning Wind in the lead, their bows drawn full. Buffalo Tail and He Who Spits, both larger men, trail a short way behind.

Hiding Rabbit shoots first, a good shot in the chest that fells the buffalo almost immediately. Hiding Rabbit jumps to the ground and taps the horns with his bow, crying out, "*Ah-heh!*" You now know that the words mean "I claim it," but hearing them shouted out calls to mind the morning of your capture and your father dying beneath just such a triumphant cry of victory.

Morning Wind's bull is struck behind the shoulder, but the arrow does not penetrate more than half its length. The enraged buffalo turns and plows into Morning Wind's horse, goring it with its deadly horns, causing it to rear and topple

over dead. Leaping to his feet, Morning Wind looses his arrow straight into the chest of the charging animal. It pauses, shakes its great head, and dies.

Now the women are racing down the hill, shouting wildly. This is a time of great joy for them. There will be food for the whole village for days. The butchering begins on the spot. Spring Flower slits open the buffalo's throat, and Coyote Eyes catches the blood in several small pots and buffalo-stomach water bags. These are handed around to the hunters, who drink the warm liquid, some of it spilling over their chins and onto their chests. This doesn't bother you as much as you expect it to, since you have gotten

used to some pretty strange eating habits already. Still, you try not to watch.

Next, the skin is cut down the backbone, making sure that the tendons are left intact. Bee Woman removes these gently. Dried and shredded, they will make thread and bow strings and other small cords. Huge steaks are taken out and laid on a skin flat on the ground. Finally the Comanche delicacy is removed —the liver. Coyote Eyes splashes green gall over it, and Spring Flower slices off thick pieces of the brown meat. The first piece goes to Hiding Rabbit, who made the first kill. Then he startles everyone by offering the slice to you.

Maybe it is the fear of being ridiculed

yet again by the women for your weak stomach, and maybe it is just that everyone is watching you. Of course you realize that this is Hiding Rabbit's way of making up or being kind or generous or whatever, but it is almost more than you can stand. Still, you accept the slice of liver and take a very small bite. To your surprise more than anyone else's, you find that it is rich and sweet and not tough at all.

Turn to page 113

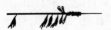

In deciding to remain, you realize that you have taken the final step in becoming one of the Nermernuh, the People. When you consider that it has been only ten weeks since your capture, you are amazed at the changes you see in yourself. But you have seen that there are two sides to life on the Texas frontier. You were always told that the land was just there for the taking. You were always told that the Indians were just barely people. "Bloodthirsty savages" was the phrase used most often. Only now do you fully realize that these "savages" are people and that to take their land means basically that these people must be exterminated. You remember the Johnson boys playing Rangers and Indians. When they played the game, there were always brave warriors fighting brave Rangers. No one ever played "massacre the village."

Yes, you tell yourself, these are primitive people. They know nothing of God or writing or even how to use a wheel. They drink blood and eat raw meat. Yes, they are violent—probably more violent than you know. They murder innocent settlers like your parents; they kill people just to steal their horses. But don't they have good reason to be so angry with the whites? Thirty years ago thousands of

Pehnahterkuhs lived all over South and West Texas. Now there are only eleven people in Buffalo Tail's band, and he says he knows of only one other band that has not been driven to the northern reservations. You remember the story of the Council House fight, which used to seem so funny. Thirteen Comanche chiefs were invited to a peace talk in San Antonio. When the chiefs were seated on the floor of a small courtroom, soldiers marched in and informed the chiefs that they were captives. Within minutes, twelve of the greatest names in Comanche history were dead.

The smoldering village and dead mothers and grandmothers and children tell you better than any history lesson that the whites do not want peace with the Indians. They want no Indians.

You mount your pony and ride to where Buffalo Tail and the others are sorting out useless tepee skins from those that can be trimmed and resewn.

"There is something my heart tells me to do," you tell him. "But I will return."

Laying one hand on your saddle horn, he says, "Do not be foolish, Singing Hawk. You cannot bring your brother back."

You shake your head and look away to where the Rangers must have gone. "I used to think white people wanted to share the land with the Indians. But now I know I was wrong," you say. "I will come back."

He is uncertain. You could lead them back. But he does not say this. Instead he says, "We will go north from here. Follow us when you have done what your heart tells you."

The Rangers' trail is easily followed. Twenty or more iron-shod horses have trampled the grass flat. You allow your pony to gallop until you see a whisp of smoke rising from a campfire. It is the Rangers' camp. You try to decide just what it is that you want to do. You hate them for killing Joey, for killing the mothers and children, and you wish that you were a warrior. But you are not. You are a twelve-year-old girl just learning to be a Comanche. But you must do something to show them . . . to show them that you reject the white man's way.

Turn to page 93

All day long you watch through the peephole, occasionally taking a shot whenever there is a movement among the trees at the edge of the yard. Christina comes out from under the bed to stand by you, handing you cartridges when you need them. She is so scared that, even though tears course down her cheeks all day, she barely says a word. When you are not watching for another attack, you must tend to Mama. The things she tells you to do are terrifying but absolutely necessary. The arrow in her shoulder, partially stuck into the bone of her shoulder blade, must be pulled out. It bleeds a little, but a wad of spider web and a cloth bandage stop it. The arrow in her leg looks like it will be easier to deal with. You break the shaft off, then slide it out. The wound is clean, but it begins to bleed freely. No matter how tight you tie them, several bandages are soaked through by evening.

Mama has you empty everything out of the small root cellar, which is really little more than a hole in the floor covered with some boards. If the Indians set fire to the cabin, she says, you and Christina will hide in the little cellar.

"If it comes to that," she tells you, "don't come out for at least a day, no matter how hot it gets, no matter what you hear, no matter what you think is going on." She makes you and Christina promise.

"If you make it that long," she tells you, "head downstream for old man Guerra's place."

Mama tries hard not to pass out with the pain, but she makes less and less sense as the day drags on. She begins talking about things that happened before you were born, talking to you as if you had been there at the time, and then she does not recognize you at all for a while. Toward mid-afternoon she finally settles down and goes to sleep. You put the last log in the cabin on the fire, check that the rifle is loaded, and sit down beside Mama and Christina on the floor. Mama wakes for a brief moment, long enough to look lovingly at you both, then murmur something that ended with "poor dears," before she nods off again. You are stiff with the cold, sad to the point of sickness, and your shoulder is bruised solid blue from the shocking recoil of the rifle. You lean against the wall next to Mama, helping support her. It seems only a few seconds have passed, but when you wake, the sun is down and it is pitch-dark outside.

Christina is shaking you. "Nancy, come

on. There's someone outside. Mama said to get in the root cellar."

"Not just yet," you reply, still a little sleepy. Then you sit up with a start. Mama, warm and loving and playful Mama, feels strange next to you. As you get up, she tips silently over onto the floor. She is dead.

The fire is stone cold, and only a little light is cast by the moon. Its cold white light slips through some of the cracks in the roof, casting long jagged white lines on the dirt floor. Christina starts to cry again, burying her head in Mama's lap.

"Shhhh," you tell her, and she tries to stifle her crying with her apron. Outside, you hear footsteps—stealthy, just a hint of movement. Going to the peephole, you can see a Comanche brave just in front of the house. You raise the rifle to the hole.

"Christina," you whisper, "get into the cellar."

Several braves are outside now, milling about, talking together. Then you hear the crackle of flames as another Comanche approaches carrying a torch. They're going to set the cabin on fire! You look at Mama, lying on the floor, and remember the promise you made to hide in the cellar. But should you keep it? You can kill one or two of the Indians who killed your mother and father. They are easy targets. Maybe they won't fire the cabin if you start shooting. If you can just hold them off through the night, maybe old man Guerra will hear the shots and bring some help. It is confusing, but you try hard to think clearly. If you do shoot and they break in or burn down the cabin, will they know someone besides Mama was alive inside? Surely they saw you run into the cabin, but since you did not make any noise while you were asleep, will they think you escaped somehow? Christina is whispering for you to come to the cellar. Will they know to look for a cellar? You are so angry and sad and confused all at the same time. What should you do?

If you decide to fight, turn to page 11

If you decide to hide in the cellar, turn to page 39

The village is not at all what you had imagined an Indian encampment to be. One time you saw a drawing of one in the San Antonio newspaper. It showed long lines of neat, highly decorated tepees, with a big fire in the middle and lots of warriors wearing big feather bonnets sitting around it. You count only nine dwellings in this camp. There are a couple of large tepees near the center, both of which have an earthen-red border painted around their bottoms and an animal or two drawn on the sides. The other tepees are smaller and have no decoration — unless you could call a few patches here and there decorations. Beyond these are a variety of lean-to shelters made of branches and buffalo skins. Wisps of smoke are coming from the tops of most of the tepees, but only one or two cooking fires are in the open. And finally, no one is wearing a feather bonnet. Shaggy Bull and Buffalo Tail both wore some sort of bonnet with buffalo horns and a few hanging feathers, but they take them off once they enter the camp.

The little camp is next to a small creek. There are only a few twisted trees, all of which lean markedly to the south, the effect of the almost continuous northern winds during the winter. Buffalo Tail tells

you and Joey to sit down and remain under one of these trees, while some sort of council is held about you. In the meantime, nine children—all there are in the village—come to gawk at you. They appear wilder to you than the adults do, skinny to the point that their bones show, with protruding bellies and black, black eyes. They remind you, in fact, of the starving and skittish deer that sometimes approached the cabin when Mama made bread.

The children, all younger than you, wear whatever they can find in winter. Among the girls, there are buckskin shirts, knee-high moccasins, short leather skirts, and a buckskin dress or two, some of which are decorated with paint or beadwork. The boys wear the knee-high moccasins, buckskin shirts, and nothing else. When it gets *really* cold, they will all muffle themselves up in furry buffalo robes. You sit still while they feel the cloth of your dress, run their fingers through your hair, tap on the hard soles of Joey's boots and pull at his denim pants, satisfying their curiosity. Then a call from the central tepee sends them running.

After a while, Buffalo Tail comes and cuts your wrists loose. "Come now," he says. "We see who you belong to." The simple act of stretching your arms out feels so luxurious that you are sure you will be grateful to the old man forever. It is a feeling you cut off with a conscious effort.

You and Joey sit side by side near a fire, over which the haunch of an antelope is roasting. An old woman with a deeply creased face and short gray hair sits turning the spit every so often. She is Bee Woman, Buffalo Tail's first wife. She reaches over and pats Joey's knee, saying something in her own strange language to him. On the trail, you had nothing to eat but pemmican—a mixture of dried meat, nuts, berries, and buffalo grease. The smell of fresh meat cooking is overwhelming.

Buffalo Tail is, in this small band, the *par-riah-boh,* the civil chief. For this raid, Shaggy Bull had been the war chief, but his authority held only outside the village. The five warriors who captured you and Joey are the only adult males left in the band. Considering that of their few adult warriors, two were killed on the raid, you would think that this would make them very sad. But to the contrary, they seem excited and pleased with the results. You ask Buffalo Tail about this, and to your very great relief he tells you that the two dead warriors were not from this band, not even Pehnahterkuh, but two wandering Mutsani Comanches from the north. They had taunted Buffalo Tail that the Pehnahterkuh were no longer the fierce raiders that they once had been, so he had invited them to go raiding with them.

"Too bad they die," he says, "but little sorrow to people here."

As civil chief, Buffalo Tail has the responsibility to divide up the spoils of the raid. The food is first. Mama's bags of sugar and coffee are divided evenly among the families. Among the Comanches, these are great delicacies that will be used sparingly over several months. The smoked meats and sausages that Father had cured are distributed as well and eaten as they are handed out. Mama's skillet and pans are given to the most needy among the band.

"I feel like I ought to be angry," Joey says to you, "seeing all Mama's things handed out like this. But I don't really feel angry—more just sad."

"I know what you mean. They are so poor, and, well, they all look sort of sick," you reply. "I wonder why there are so few of them? I always thought that there were thousands and thousands of Indians out here."

"These are Pehnahterkuh, and Father told me that the reason we were pretty safe by the Frio was that the Pehnahterkuh had been mostly killed off a long time ago."

"I remember," you tell him. "Father told us about the battle of Plum Creek, where the Rangers killed a thousand Pehnahterkuhs—and the thirteen chiefs killed in the Council House fight in San Antonio were Pehnahterkuhs as well."

"But that was thirty years ago," says Joey. "You don't think that this is all that's left of the tribe, do you?"

You don't know the answer to that. You do know that the Pehnahterkuhs were once the biggest and meanest single group of all the Comanches. Their name means "Honey Eaters." They had lived in the Hill Country and all over South Texas before the settlers, Rangers, and soldiers drove them west out onto the open plains. This just might be the last of them. You decide to ask Buffalo Tail about that later.

In the meantime, everything has been divided up except for a few odds and ends—Father's watch, his pocketknife—which Buffalo Tail is giving as special presents to the warriors who went on the raid with him. The last thing he pulls from the saddle bag is your flute. Your flute!

You jump up and reach for it, but Buffalo Tail pushes you away and two women force you to sit down again.

Buffalo Tail looks closely at the flute, then at you. He seems to ask a question of the group, but no one replies. Finally he turns to you. "What is it?" he asks.

"A flute," you say, holding your hands up as if you were playing it.

Buffalo Tail holds it as you indicate, but he has no idea what it does. Slowly you get up, looking at the chief to see if it is all right, then you put out your hands.

"It is a flute. It makes music," you say. Slowly, and with some misgiving, Buffalo Tail hands you the flute. Later you will find out that the Comanches make and play whistles of several different kinds, some of which have a nice tone but only three or four notes. They have never seen this sort of instrument before. You put it to your lips as the circle of observers widens. All that comes to mind for you to play is one song. The words take on a new and special meaning for you as the melody soars: "Amazing grace, how sweet the sound . . . "

The Comanches are enchanted, then curious. The children and then the adults gather around you to touch the flute, to hold it, and finally almost everyone in the village tries blowing into it, though no one succeeds in making any music. Buffalo Tail quiets them all after a while, then makes a very long speech. He seems to you to be reciting the whole raid from beginning to end, occasionally pointing to you or Joey or to Father's big bay mare or to another of the items taken. His speech is almost like music, rising and falling in melodic phrases, and everyone listens intently until he finishes. In English, he tells you that he has just given you a new name for a "girl fighter who sings through stick." The name is a long one, even for Comanches, and it is gradually shortened. In the end, you are called "Singing Hawk."

Turn to page 23

You wait until the darkest hour between sunset and moonrise before you approach the camp. Most of the Rangers are already asleep, but a few sit near the fire, drinking coffee and talking. Their horses are tethered at the edge of the camp. Now you know what you must do—there is nothing more purely Comanche than stealing horses. One at a time, you untie a horse and lead it quietly down the hill to where your pony is waiting. When you have a dozen, you link them by tying the reins of one horse to the reins of the next. One last time you approach the camp. You cut off a lock of your hair and tie it to the rope to which the horses had been tethered. They will know from the color of your hair who took their horses.

Silently, you walk the horses west as the moon rises behind you. By the time you arrive at the deserted village, the moon is high in the sky, its white light falling harshly on the dark bundles held aloft in the leafless arms of the trees along the creek. You say farewell to Joey and ride north.

Just before sunrise, you come upon Buffalo's new camp, which consists of a single lodge constructed of too few poles and barely enough skins to keep the wind off the sleepers inside. They too have traveled most of the night, burdened down with meat from yesterday's hunt and the salvaged items from the village. You tie the horses beside the lodge and sit down in front of the door to wait for the dawn.

Turn to page 147

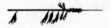

It is Hiding Rabbit! You recognize him now. You remember the embarrassment of having your dress torn off. You remember his hands. You leap out of your hiding place onto his back, wrapping your left arm around his neck and stabbing with your right. You know you struck a good blow—you could feel it in the knife handle—but suddenly Hiding Rabbit has twisted beneath your grip and thrown you to the ground. In an instant he is on top of you. Your knife flies into the grass as he pins your arms down and butts your head with his own. Pulling your arms together, he rips some long fringes off of his war shirt and wraps them around your wrists.

He yanks you to your feet but staggers himself with the effort. He is bleeding freely from where you stabbed him in the chest. Kicking free you begin to run, but Hiding Rabbit follows. You hear the twang of his bowstring and then a hideous pain in your back. "Run, Joey," you think, and then you know no more.

End

You tell Joey to wait with the others at the circle hunt while you return to the tepee. Going over to Spring Flower, you complain that you are cold and that you are going to get a robe from the camp. Even in the short time since your capture, you have learned a few Comanche words, including those for "cold," "robe," and "camp." Spring Flower laughs, then returns her attention to the direction from which the antelope will appear.

In camp you have no trouble finding a couple of warm buffalo robes, a skin sack full of pemmican, a water bag (made from a buffalo stomach lining), a couple of small flints, and a knife. Last, you pick up an old pair of Buffalo Tail's moccasins— and your flute. Wrapping yourself in the robe, you quickly run back to the circle hunt.

Joey is at the edge of the circle, as excited as anyone. Soon the lead antelope comes prancing and leaping into sight. When the circle is full of the excited animals, everyone begins shouting as the open end of the circle is closed. Finally Dancing Moon gives the signal and everyone rushes in. If you did not have a hand on Joey's shoulder, he too would have joined the fray.

"Quickly," you say. "While no one is looking."

Together you work your way down toward the mouth of the shallow draw where the kill is going on and then run across the open prairie until you reach the stunted trees along the creek.

"This is no good," says Joey. "They can follow us down the creek without any problem at all."

"I know. That's why we're here. Your boots leave clear tracks, so walk along this side of the creek until you come to those stepping stones. Then cross over on them. Then get on my back, and I'll carry you away from the stream. Maybe then they will think we waded down the stream to lose them."

"Nancy, even a Comanche wouldn't go wading in this weather!"

"They would if their life depended on it."

Going ahead of Joey, you cross the stream first on the stones, then, while Joey balances on the last one, you take a stick and dislodge the two behind him so that they roll a few feet downstream.

"With the stones that far apart," you say, "at least they will be looking for wet tracks."

"Hurry up, Nancy," says your little

brother. "I'm going to fall in, and then there *will* be wet tracks."

"Just one more thing," you say. Pulling out the old pair of Buffalo Tail's moccasins, you slip your feet, boots and all, into the larger footwear. Comanche men wear long fringes and sometimes animal tails trailing behind their moccasins. These have two wolf tails on each. Finally you get Joey up on your back. With the wolf-tail moccasins and with Joey on your back, you hope the Comanches will overlook your tracks for those of a male warrior.

"Let's go," you say.

The sounds of the antelope kill fade as you carefully walk into the high plains grass, trying to step down as little of the grass as possible, heading due east. If you are lucky, you think, you will not be missed until sometime during the feasting after the hunt. You might have a whole hour's head start. After you are a good distance away from the stream, you begin to run, gaining as much distance as you can. You run until your back and legs ache beyond standing. Stopping to rest, you put Joey down, take off Buffalo Tail's moccasins, and have Joey put them on over his hard-soled shoes. Then both of you begin to run, bending low to keep your heads below the level of the grass. By late afternoon, you are exhausted and must stop to rest.

Joey admires the way you have managed the escape so far. "Nancy, you sure learned alot while you were a Comanche," he says.

"Shhh," you caution him. Then whispering, you say, "I never was a Comanche, and I never want to be one."

Joey stuffs some grass into his headband and then stands up. "Something *I* learned," he says. "This way I'll just look like a tall weed. Get down on your hands

and knees so I can stand on your back."

"What do you see?" you ask after he has been there for a minute or more.

Slowly, he lowers himself straight down, then gets off. "They know we are gone," he says. "It looks like there are two or three riders zigzagging through the grass about a mile back. It's hard to tell, they are so far off."

"It will be dark in a couple of hours," you say. "Are they that far away?"

"I don't know. Maybe we better keep moving. Something else," Joey says. "Up ahead of us a few miles there is a rocky-looking hill. It would be harder to track us across rocky ground."

Your legs and back ache, and you are very hungry. If you are going to go any further before nightfall, you will have to do it now, because the western light of the sun will show movement more easily for a while before sunset. Or you can hide here without moving until dark. If the scouts are zigzagging, then they have not picked up your trail. They could give up and go elsewhere, but even if they do not, finding you in the tall grass should be pretty difficult—unless they find your trail. Munching on some of the pemmican and drinking a little of the funny-tasting water, you consider the problem.

*Do you rest until nightfall or go on?
If you decide to continue, go on to
the next page.*

*If you decide to wait until nightfall,
turn to page 127*

Y ou decide that, as tired as you are, distance is your best defense. Carefully, you begin walking east again, crouching low to keep your heads below the level of the grass. After an hour or so, you risk letting Joey climb on your back again to see if you are being followed.

"There's no one there at all," he reports, "unless they are following us on foot. I wouldn't be able to see them at all then." This thought has already crossed your mind.

"Joey, I don't think it is really even *possible* for them to miss our trail. Buffalo Tail said that a Comanche could follow a day-old rabbit's trail if it was necessary. Surely they are following us."

"As for the rabbit," says Joey, "I've seen them do it. The only thing they can't follow is a scent, and I'm not sure of that. The question is, did the moccasin trick fool them?"

"I just can't believe it would fool them for very long," you say. "I am sure they are behind us. Maybe we had better split up."

"No, let's just keep going."

"There's only a little light left," you say, "and the moon will be up soon. Do we run or keep walking? I'm getting stiff with the cold, and the wind is moving the grass enough that we might not be seen."

If you decide to run, turn to page 153

*If you decide to continue at a slow
pace, turn to page 137*

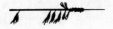

You remember how angry you were at Hiding Rabbit that first day—how embarrassed you were when your dress was torn off. Still, despite your desire to escape, you cannot bring youself to kill him. The big knife trembles in your hand, and you try not to breathe.

Suddenly he turns and 'strides back through the grass. That means there are no other warriors near or he would simply have called to them. Within a few minutes, you are sure that he has returned to camp. Did he not look for you anymore because he liked you and knew that if he found you he might have to kill you? Or is he just returning to camp to get horses and more warriors?

Ignoring caution, you race toward the rising moon and the hill where Joey will be waiting. The band knows the trail and which way you are going, so your only salvation now is to try to lose them again and to get out of Comancheria as quickly as possible.

Frozen with the night air, burdened down with the heavy buffalo robe, and exhausted from running and from the nerve-tingling brush with Hiding Rabbit, you reach the hill at about the same time Joey does. He has been taking his time, leaving as clean a trail as possible.

"They know where we are," you gasp to him. "We've got to run for it."

Whenever possible, you walk on top of the larger rocks as you skirt the bottom of the hill, then keep to rocky soil as far as it extends into the plain beyond. Once in the grass again, it is all you can do to keep walking. Joey is impressed with your courage for waiting to see if anyone was following your trail, but angry with you for having risked your life for his. You do not tell him how close you came to fighting it out with Hiding Rabbit right there. If you had tried, you might be dead right now. You are so tired, you think, "I might as well be dead." To Joey, you say, "We've got to find a place to hide for a while. I just can't go any further."

"You've got to Nancy. Just keep going, and we'll find some place to rest."

The rest of the night, you keep putting one foot in front of the other, but find yourself dozing off while you are walking. In your mind, you hear your father's warnings about the Indians again: "If you see an Indian, don't stop running until you see me. If you see an Indian, don't stop running until you see me."

"I'm coming, Father," you say right out loud, startling Joey.

"I know," he says sympathetically.

"You're tired. We've got to rest."

A little before sunrise, you come to a small wood that extends to the top of a fairly tall hill. Making your way carefully through the trees, you pick your way up the hill until at last you reach the top.

Wrapping yourselves up in the buffalo robes, you both lie down and sleep like logs. Whether or not Buffalo Tail's band followed you that morning ou will never know, for it is well after noon when the two of you begin to stir. The ground is dusted with a half-inch of snow.

To the west, nothing is moving—and from the top of the hill, you can see a very long way. You must have walked miles during the night. That is not something you have to tell your feet. They are a mass of blisters, and your toes are stiff and red with frostbite.

Go on to next page

"**I**f you think we are safe here," you say, "we might stay another night. I am not sure I can go very far on these feet."

Joey leaves you on top of the hill to go look for a sheltered spot. When he returns, you hobble down to a small cave opening, really little more than a over-hanging rock. The snow makes it difficult to find dry wood, but Joey does his best. You bring out the flints you took from the tepee and the knife. Joe produces a small leather pouch from which he takes a bit of black cloth.

"Little Smile gave me this bag," he explains. "It has some herbs, some leather thongs, and this cloth rubbed with gunpowder."

You cover the little piece of cloth with some dry grass and several small twigs and shavings from a larger piece of wood. A few strokes of the back of the knife blade on the flint procudes a spark that ignites the cloth. Soon you have a small blaze, which Joey feeds with wood and a few antelope chips. On top of it all he places a dozen or so small stones.

When the stones are hot, he drops them into the buffalo-stomach water bag, along with the herbs. "Drink this," he tells you. "Little Smile said it helps ease pain."

The warm drink and warming your feet

at the fire put you to sleep again. When you awake, it is morning, and there is more snow. You can feel your toes now, and they feel like they are on fire. Still, you know that you must go on. There is no more pemmican left, and you will have to melt snow for water. It will be a cold march after tomorrow night you think. Joey has only a small piece of the fire cloth left, and you are not at all sure you can strike a fire without it.

To the east, the wood around this hill extends only another mile or so, where it gives way to open prairie again. You might survive here for a while, but it would only get more difficult. Soon you are on your way.

The Comanches call this part of late winter the Moon of Babies Crying for Food. You understand that now, as hunger soon begins gnawing at your stomach. All day long you walk across a prairie of snow and grass, brooding that you will probably die here, either of starvation or of exposure.

"I must have heard a dozen stories about people dying on the prairies in the wintertime," you tell Joey.

"The Comanches didn't seem to mind winter too much," he replies, his words hanging like his breath in the air.

"That's it!" you say. "I'm sorry I told you

that I was never a Comanche. Here we are already thinking like white people again when thinking like Comanches will keep us alive."

After that, things go easier. Pretty soon you find an old buffalo horn to carry coals from one fire to the next. And there is plenty of nopal—prickly-pear cactus leaves that are as good as bread. The *yep,* what some people called "Indian potato," is easily spotted, and the leather thongs from Little Smile's bag prove just right to snare a few rabbits along the way. By keeping your feet dry, and not walking too far each day, the trip east goes almost easily.

Twenty-one days after escaping from the Comanches, you come to the top of a hill overlooking a freshly plowed field. At the other end of the field, a farmer drops the reins from his mule and takes aim at you with a big Sharps Carbine.

"Wait!" you both cry out, running toward him and waving.

He holds his aim for a moment, then puts down the gun. Later, in his warm cabin, while you are gobbling up hot beans and cornbread, he tells you, "Hadn't been for that yeller hair of yours, girl, you'd both be dead Comanches."

End

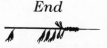

The butchering is over in a couple of hours. The meat is wrapped carefully in skins and, along with the useful bones and horns, loaded onto the pack horses. The strange odor that Hiding Rabbit mentioned must have blown away, and the odd behavior of the buffalo is forgotten during the joyful ride back to camp. Hiding Rabbit, so bold after your capture and so shy ever since, rides beside you, smiling. By eating the raw liver, you seem to have crossed some boundary—both for yourself and for the others. Some change has occurred, and you feel closer to these people. At the same time, you hate yourself for it. They are murderers, you tell yourself, savages. Yet at the same time you must admit that they are both proud and innocent. It is confusing.

There is yelling up ahead, and you look to see what the commotion is about. Coyote Eyes is pointing across the plains in the direction of the camp. You sit up, shade your eyes against the noon sun, and see a small column of dark smoke. They must be making some cooking fire, you think at first, but that doesn't make sense. It would be wasting precious wood, and wood smoke is not that color anyway. Something is wrong. Very wrong. You sense it in the column of smoke and in the voices around you. Without further words, everyone is galloping toward camp.

You are no match for the others when it comes to riding. Both men and women seem to be more at home on horseback than on foot, and they outdistance you easily. Before you top the small rise just north of the camp, you have no idea what you will see. You have heard of houses or cabins catching fire, but never a tepee. But that is the only thing big enough to cause the smoke, you think. When the village comes into sight, however, you are horrified.

All the tepees, all the shelters, even the little sweat lodge, have been pulled down, piled together with their poles, and set on fire. Throughout the camp, old men, women, and children lie with their limbs sprawled out. Something terrible has happened. You ride on into camp and dismount where the others are gathered around Shaggy Bull. The warrior has been shot several times—and scalped—but he is still alive, hanging on through will alone to tell his chief what happened. The first thought that crosses your mind is that Shaggy Bull has been paid back for what he did to your father, but that thought is wiped out by sudden concern for Joey. A few survivors are beginning to come out of hiding, but there are no wounded. You run from one body to the next, finding each has been shot more than once, some close enough to show round black burn spots from the gunpowder. Little Smile and her daughter lie together in a heap in front of where their small lodge had stood. Blood is everywhere. A little way beyond them are three bodies lying in the grass. You run to them. There, with his bow and a dead rabbit still clutched in his hand, lies Joey. You cradle his lifeless body and wail until you are hoarse.

In all, there are only three survivors, an old man and his wife and one small child. There are 24 dead. Exactly two thirds of Buffalo Tail's band has been wiped out. Even as the story is pieced together, the ritual mourning begins. The women claw at their breasts or slash their arms with knives, tearing at their hair and screaming until some fall senseless. Your grief is as deep, yet your anger is even stronger. "Who did this?" you demand of the survivors, who stare mutely at you, not understanding a word. "Who?" you demand of Buffalo Tail. "Which one of your noble enemies did this?"

"Rangers," he says quietly.

At first you cannot believe him. White

people do not kill women and children, you think. Rangers do not scalp Comanches. No, it is the other way around. But the full impact of the tragedy begins to reach you as you try to grapple with this nonsensical fact. Rangers did do this. Yes, somewhere you have heard that settlers are actually paid for Indian scalps. Yes, you remember stories of Indian villages being burned. You just never realized that people, Nermernuh, real people died. And Joey, Joey who wasn't even one of the people, they killed Joey too. Your anger rises like an uncontrolled boiling within you. How dare they? What right did they have? Why?

The answer reduces your anger to a sickening stillness. The Rangers were trying to save *you*. All these people died because of you—poor little white girl captured by the Comanches. The thought drives you crazy. You want it not to be true. It is hours before Bee Woman and Spring Flower can calm your hysterical sobbing.

Sick and almost blind with sorrow, you help the remaining members of the band drag the dead to the trees beside the creek. Each body is wrapped in a buffalo robe, though most of the robes are badly singed. Then you place the bodies high in the limbs of the trees, halfway between earth and sky, away from any animals that might bother them on the ground.

The Comanches, so independent that they cannot even be called a single tribe, do not worship a single Great Spirit. The people pass from the hard world of buffalo and grass to a spirit world of which they know nothing. It is the personal medicine, the spirit world guardian of each man or woman that will see them into the next world. There are no rituals or ceremonies, just the mourning of the women and the anger of the warriors.

You help pick through the smoldering ruins of the camp, looking for items that can be salvaged — a pot, a tepee pole, a few tepee skins, cracked and blackened but still usable. Among the rubble, you find things that you recognize from Buffalo Tail's lodge, such as a beaded arrow quiver, so brittle that when you pick it up all the beads tumble to the ground. There is Bee Woman's grinding stone for crushing mesquite beans. The fire has cracked it. Finally, there is a charred piece of cane. You pick up the flute and watch as most of it turns to ashes in your hand.

While this is going on, the warriors debate whether or not to follow the Rangers, whose track is still clearly visible.

Before Shaggy Bull died, he told of some thirty Rangers and other white men who galloped into camp, shooting anything that moved. The women do not want the warriors to go. The band cannot afford the loss of any more life, especially any warriors. This is not the time for raids or vengeance. That will come later, they say. This is the time to worry about shelter. About the survival of the band.

You are not at all sure where you belong in this world. Mama and Father are dead at the hands of the Comanches. Joey is dead at the hands of the whites. And Christina, what of Christina? She must be alive, since it would have been she who brought the news of your capture to old man Guerra. How would she take knowing that her efforts to rescue you had ended with Joey's death?

Your horse stands nearby, saddled and ready. The trail of the Rangers is clear. You could probably catch up with them by nightfall. Where do you belong? Your yellow hair tells everyone that you are not truly one of the Nermernuh, yet you have eaten the raw buffalo liver. The only blood relative you have left in the world is a helpless little girl who probably has nightmares every night of *that* night. Do you go to Christina, or do you remain with the Nermernuh?

If you decide to follow the Rangers, turn to page 17

If you decide to remain, turn to page 75

For three years the band wanders, hunting the buffalo, but finding smaller and smaller herds and more and more piles of bones. Occasionally you meet other Comanche bands, but everywhere the story is the same: White hunters have slaughtered the herds, Bluecoat soldiers have slaughtered villages. Wanderers, separated from their traditional bands by death or necessity, join your band now and then, until Buffalo Tail is the civil chief of a small village of six tepees.

One of the young braves who has joined the band is Tall Feather. One morning you awake to find six horses tied outside of Buffalo Tail's tent. Spring Flower at first teases you that Hiding Rabbit is finally ready to marry you, but it soon becomes clear that six horses is the price offered for Spring Flower, not you, and that they are offered by Tall Feather.

Buffalo Tail accepts the horses, and Spring Flower moves her robes into Tall Feather's tepee. You are surprised that there is no more to a Nermernuh wedding that that, and it is lonely without Spring Flower to talk to in the evenings. You watch her joy with something like envy and begin to get impatient with Hiding Rabbit. Many evenings you spend walking with Hiding Rabbit, talking and talking, yet still he does not make an offer of horses to Buffalo Tail.

But it is not a good time for thinking of the future. The present is hard enough. The buffalo grow fewer. The people are hungry, and neither earth nor sky takes pity on the Nermernuh. Droughts are followed by floods, and always there is the danger of soldiers. The Rangers to the south were bad but few in number; the Bluecoat soldiers here in the north are many, and they shoot rifles that never need loading. No warrior with spear and shield, arrow and knife, can stand up to them. Every village has more widows and orphans than warriors.

There is a deep fear everywhere among the people, and no chief can tell you how to live with that fear. The Bluecoat soldiers want all the Nermernuh to move onto the reservation lands to the east in Oklahoma. They want you to live in houses like the whites, teach your children to read like the whites, plant seeds in the ground like the whites. Despite your yellow hair, life on the reservation sounds like death.

Then suddenly there is hope. A prophet rises among the Nermernuh, a *puhakut* whose medicine is strong. His name is Ishatai, Coyote Droppings, and people say he is immune to bullets. Did he not predict the comet last summer and the drought that followed? Everywhere is talk of nothing but Ishatai and his plan to bring all the Nermernuh together. The comet, he says, was a sign from the Great Spirit, who told Ishatai that the Nermernuh have too long wandered like lost children, with one band going here and another there. To defeat the white man, the Nermernuh must forget that they are Pehnahterkuh or Nokoni, Kwerharrehnuh or Yampahreekun—all are Nermernuh. If all the Nermernuh come together, says Ishatai, and perform the sacred Sun Dance of the Kiowas and Cheyennes, then the Great Spirit will protect them from the white soldier's bullets. When the white man has been driven from the land, the Great Spirit promises to replenish the buffalo.

Buffalo Tail is impressed but not convinced. The Pehnahterkuh, once the largest of all Nermernuh bands, now number in the tens rather than in the thousands. The other bands, he says, know neither the real power nor the treachery of the White man. The old chief launches into one of his lengthy speeches, ending it by saying:

Turn to page 131

Only when the sun is almost completely gone do you risk letting Joey climb on your back again to look for the scouts. He reports that nothing is moving that he can see. You too look long and hard into the sunset, but there are no horsemen to be seen. You knew that your trick at the stream would slow them up, but you did not expect the Comanches to be unable to find your trail at all. Something about that thought makes you nervous.

"Joey," you whisper into his ear. "Maybe they did find the trail. Maybe they are following it on foot." Together you peer into the dark forest of grass stems that were only a short time ago a friendly yellow sea.

"We'd better split up," you whisper. "We'll take two different routes to that rocky hill you saw. I'll meet you there sometime tonight, but if I'm not there by morning, go on without me." Kissing him on the forehead, you push him in the direction you want him to take.

Turning around for a moment, he says, "Good luck, Nancy." Then he is gone into the grass.

You will need the luck, you think, as you have no intention of leaving right away. If they are trailing you and they come this far, they will find you but not Joey. You crawl into the thickest part of the grass to wait, tense and watching.

Turn to page 133

For years you remain uncertain about your decision to return to San Antonio. The Rangers did indeed go out the next day and track down the remnant of Buffalo Tail's band. They were fleeing north, looking for other Comanches. The Rangers report leaving eleven Comanches dead on the prairie, so you know that no one escaped.

Christina recognizes you, but remains mute for the rest of her short life. Most of the time she just sits in a chair, staring at the street outside the McAllens' front window. At the age of twelve, just the age you were when you were captured, Christina falls ill during a cholera epidemic and dies.

Even though you survive the experience, you never really get over it. Fifty years later, you have seen San Antonio grow from a dusty little town to a bustling city. You watched as cars became more common than horses and airplanes fly overhead everyday. Yet of all the things you have seen in your life, the one experience you most enjoy telling children about—and the one they most want to hear about over and over—is your ten weeks with the Comanches. You tell them about Spring Flower and Bee Woman, who taught you to mend tepees and butcher buffalo; about Dancing Moon, whose medicine was never strong enough; about Buffalo Tail and his knowledge of the land; and about Hiding Rabbit, whom you think you might have married if you had stayed among the Nermernuh, the People. You wonder quite often what would have happened if instead of going to sleep that night so long ago, you had taken your pony and ridden west.

End

"Other *puhakuts* promised such things in the past. Warriors followed them in war paint and faith — and died in war paint and faith. The Nermernuh have never prayed to the Great Spirit of the Cheyennes and Arapahos; we do not carry their sacred bundles; our *puhakuts* are not priests — they are only men who have seen further than others into the spirit world. Why should their Great Spirit come to aid us now — *after* we have suffered so much? There are too few Pehnahterkuhs left to waste them on the dreams of a madman. This is not our path."

Still, some members of Buffalo Tail's band will not listen. They would rather die fighting than lose hope, so they ignore the old chief's words of warning and head north to join Ishatai and dance the Sun Dance and attack the whites. Buffalo Tail leads what is left of the band south, back across the Red River.

Turn to page 135

You do not have long to wait. Less than half an hour after Joey leaves you, there is a slight rustle in the grass. You watch intently. The moon is only half full, but it is bright enough to make out the form of a man, stooping to examine the grass stems in the dim light. From underneath the buffalo robe, you pull out the knife you took from Buffalo Tail's tepee. The Comanche before you has an arrow notched to his bowstring. He carries the bow with the arrow at the ready in his left hand. With his right he fingers a grass stem as he examines it. Fortunately, you can tell that this is not Buffalo Tail. Even if the chief was part of the raid that killed your parents, he has been very kind to you since. You hope it is Shaggy Bull. You hope Joey is far enough away not to hear this. You hope there are no other warriors in the grass.

Moving more silently than ought to be possible for a human, the warrior suddenly straightens up. He has heard something. Maybe he heard Joey. He turns. His back is toward you. He is only three feet away. It is Hiding Rabbit!

If you decide to attack Hiding Rabbit,
turn to page 95

If you decide to wait it out,
turn to page 105

There, beside the slow waters of the Red River on a spring morning a few days before your sixteenth birthday, you awake to the chuckling and singing of Bee Woman and Coyote Eyes.

"What is it?" you ask, but they only laugh.

Outside the tepee, you find thirteen ponies tied in a row. Buffalo Tail is shaking his head. "She Who Steals Some Horses," he says to you very formally, "Do you know why Hiding Rabbit has taken so long to ask for you to move your robes to his tent?"

"No, Buffalo Tail," you say. "Why is that?"

With a gleam in his eye, he says, "For his own honor, he had to offer more horses for you than you stole for me!"

You begin gathering your things, but before you are ready Hiding Rabbit approaches you and Buffalo Tail.

"I must tell you," he says, "that as soon as we are married, we will go to join Ishatai for the Sun Dance. My name has been Hiding Rabbit, but I will hide no more. I am a Nermernuh warrior, and She Who Steals Some Horses and I will go join those who will drive the white man from our lands."

You too are excited by the promises of

Ishatai, and the great gathering of the bands at the Sun Dance sounds thrilling. But you have long respected the wisdom of Buffalo Tail. But he offers no counsel now. This is your decision.

If you decide to stay with Buffalo Tail, turn to page 141

If you decide to go with Hiding Rabbit, turn to page 159

You decide that the last thing you should do is run. Even if the Comanches are on your trail, they will be hard-pressed to follow it in the dark. Besides, they know this country much better than you do. If they do know that you are in this part of the prairie, they will probably figure out that you are headed toward the rocky hill to the east. Your best chance lies in moving as quietly as possible. Running, even while crouching down, would be like a flag moving in the grass to any Comanche scout who might be looking.

For an hour or so after sundown, it is very dark. Then the moon, half full, rises in the east. It is well past midnight when you come to the end of the prairie grass. Before you stretches a couple of hundred yards of stony ground without a bit of cover.

"Come on," says Joey. "Let's get to the cover of those boulders."

"Wait," you whisper. "They could already be here. They could be waiting for us."

After a half an hour, with nothing moving, you must make a decision. Do you work your way around the hill, keeping to the cover of the grass, or do you try to seek shelter among the boulders littering the base of the hill?

*If you decide to head directly for the
hill, turn to page 143*

*If you decide to go around, go on
to the next page*

Slowly, you back into the thicker grass, then begin working your way south, going counterclockwise around the hill. One quarter of the way around, you see them. Hidden among the larger boulders, you see the hindquarters of a pinto pony gleaming white in the moonlight. A little farther around, and you can see three or four mounted warriors. If you had run for the hill, you would be dead by now.

"That's all of them, don't you think?" asks Joey quietly.

"Yes, I think so. But we're not home free yet. If they wait for sunrise, they'll pick up our trail for sure. All we can do now is to keep going."

Sometimes running, sometimes trotting, but mostly walking, you are so tired that it is all you can do to keep putting one foot in front of the other. The cold has numbed your feet, and whenever you adjust the buffalo robe, the wind slices right through you. In the back of your mind, you hear your father's voice repeating, "If you see an Indian, don't stop running until you see me." You fall in step with the voice.

"I'm coming, Father," you say once out loud from the dream, startling Joey.

"It's okay, Nancy," he says. "I know how you feel."

A little before sunrise, you come to a small wood, which extends to the top of a fairly tall hill. Making your way carefully through the trees, you pick your way up the hill until at last you reach the top.

"At least from here," says Joey, "we'll be able to see anyone following us."

Wrapping yourselves up in the buffalo robes, you both lie down and sleep like logs. Whether or not Buffalo Tail's band followed you that morning you will never know, for it is well after noon when the two of you begin to stir, and the ground is dusted with a half-inch of snow.

To the west, nothing is moving—and from the top of the hill, you can see a very long way. You must have walked miles during the night. That is not something you have to tell your feet. They are a mass of blisters, and your toes are stiff and red with frostbite.

Turn to page 108

The months pass slowly without Hiding Rabbit. Tall Feather and Spring Flower travel north with him to join the Sun Dance, leaving you to help the old women keep the tepee in order. News begins to filter in a little at a time. First you learn that Ishatai brought together not only the Nermernuh but also the Kiowas and Cheyennes and Arapahos. An alliance between the tribes has never been heard of before. This fact, and their belief in Ishatai's medicine, sends more than a thousand warriors thundering south to attack the whites at a place called Adobe Walls.

Even Buffalo Tail's hopes rise when he hears of the alliance, and he prays that Ishatai's medicine is real. But Buffalo Tail, it seems, is more of a prophet than Ishatai. A handful of white hunters leave the hills around the ruins called Adobe Walls strewn with hundreds of Comanche braves.

Buffalo Tail remains in the camp on the Red River only to hear if Spring Flower, Tall Feather, and Hiding Rabbit are safe. A full month passes before Spring Flower finds her way home. The marks of grief upon her are enough. You need not ask about the others.

You begin the long journey into the rising sun the next morning. "Oklahoma is good country," says Buffalo Tail, "but it has always been home to the Kotsoteka. We will visit them, but remember, the home of the Pehnahterkuh is no more. We will pass away as surely as the buffalo."

End

"Let's run for it," you say. Quickly you and Joey cross the barren space between the grass and the rocks. Your muscles begin to relax as soon as you get moving again. It feels good to move more freely. The rocky hill, which was only a dark hump against the sky, begins to show details—trees, lots of boulders strewn about, lots of places to hide. It seems very strange to be free, as if the past weeks were a bad dream. You cannot believe it—maybe you have truly escaped. You run on, certain that no one can follow your tracks on this stony ground, until you hear the sound of horses.

"Joey," you scream. "They're ahead of us."

Four mounted warriors, two with lances and two with bows, come thundering out from behind some boulders. Before you know it, they are upon you. The only sound is the horses' hooves and the zing of an arrow. Joey falls, an arrow through his throat. You do not have to look twice to know he is dead. Pulling out Buffalo Tail's knife, you wrap the buffalo robe around your arm like a shield. Quickly you ward off one arrow, then another. You slash out at a warrior's leg, at his horse, at anything that moves.

It is Hiding Rabbit. He swings out of the saddle and faces you, lance in hand. Shaggy Bull stands behind him, your father's hair dangling from his shield. The memories of Shaggy Bull scalping your father and of your embarrassment by Hiding Rabbit rise up in your mind, and you scream out in rage and frustration as you rush them both, waving the knife.

The thrust of the lance is so quick that you barely see it. Suddenly you are lifted from the earth and as suddenly smashed to the ground. From somewhere you hear your father saying over and over again, "If

you see an Indian, don't stop running until you see me. If you see an Indian, don't stop running . . ."

"I'm running," you say. Then the stars and the moon above you fade to black.

"Singing Hawk fight like hurt bull," says Buffalo Tail, who dismounts now. "Made good Comanche."

End

The northerly wind dies to a whisper at dawn. The smell of snow is in the air, and you wait calmly as the first few flakes begin to settle around you. The quiet of falling snow on the prairie is an awesome thing—the songbirds settle into their hidden nests, the coyote snuggles into his den, even the hawk and the eagle forgo their hunting. The silence is broken only by the occasional snorts of the horses.

The snowfall grows heavier, covering the ground, weighing down the tall grass, hiding all tracks. By the time Bee Woman begins to stir—she is always the first to rise—there is no need to warn them about the Rangers' intentions. The snow has hidden all trace of your passage through the night. "The band is safe," you think, satisfied that you have made the right decision.

When Bee Woman emerges from the tent, she cries out with obvious joy, "Singing Hawk has returned!" Quickly everyone is up, welcoming you back, admiring your horses. Buffalo Tail must have been certain you would come back, for he has a speech already prepared. Your rejection of the deeds of your own people, the Rangers, proves that you have a good heart, he says. Ignoring the fact that he stole you in the first place, he tells the little group that you have come to the band as a gift. "May you be as Cynthia Ann of the Antelopes," he says in blessing, "and be the mother of many great warriors."

You are certainly not ready to be anyone's mother, you think, but you accept his words as the compliment he intended. Noting that the Rangers destroyed your flute, Buffalo Tail gives you a new name: She Who Steals Some Horses. It is a fine Comanche name, a name any woman of the Nermernuh would be proud to bear.

The band travels north for several days, your trail vanishing within minutes behind you as the snow continues to fall. Then one March day the sun rises without a cloud in the sky. By the end of the day, there is the sound of water everywhere, as the snow glistens in the sunlight and melts away. Every little gulley and ditch on the prairie turns into a raging torrent overnight, then is just as suddenly empty the following day. Spring marches across the land in waves of new green grass and sudden bursts of wildflowers.

But the thaw brings something else as well. The stench Hiding Rabbit noticed on the morning of the buffalo hunt returns. It is the odor of death, of rotting flesh. It is a common odor, but rarely so strong un-

less a dead body is very close. The stench gets worse throughout that day. Toward afternoon, something else strange occurs. There is a buzzing sound that is inexplicable because no bee swarms are in sight. The sound and the stench increase, causing everyone in the band to tremble, wondering what it is they may find.

The explanation comes late on a spring afternoon. You begin to come across the carcasses of one dead buffalo after another. They have been skinned and left to rot. It becomes clear that thousands of buffalo have been slaughtered here. The horrible lumps of decaying flesh dot the prairie in all directions for as far as the eye can see. This terrible waste of life and food appalls the Nermernuh. The idea of killing more buffalo than are needed for food is something they cannot comprehend. "Who could use so many buffalo robes?" asks Coyote Eyes, knowing full well that it was white hunters.

"This explains why the buffalo acted so strangely before," observes Hiding Rabbit. "They knew that their herd had been slaughtered. They must have thought they were the last of their kind alive."

"Like us," Dancing Moon says. "This is very bad medicine, Buffalo Tail. We must leave this place."

It takes a full two days of travel to get beyond the last rotting carcass, but the image is burned into you. The buzzing of millions of flies, the overwhelming stench that has soaked into your clothing, even into your hair and skin, the sight of vultures so gorged that they must vomit to fly so they can gorge again—these are not things easily forgotten. At the back of your mind is a nagging thought. Do the white hunters really need so many robes, or are they killing the buffalo to starve the Comanches?

Bad medicine follows you. The young boy who survived the Ranger attack has been sickly ever since. Despite Bee Woman's care and Dancing Moon's prayers, the boy dies. The old grandfather and his wife, Eagle Tail and Sweet Wind, find the depression of the buffalo slaughter so great that one morning they refuse to move. Sweet Wind explains that her husband has decided that he will die close to the spirits of so many buffalo and that she will join him.

"They can't just decide to die!" you protest to Buffalo Tail, but the chief refuses to listen. It is their decision. Apparently old people do this fairly often when they decide that they will only be a burden to the band. You leave them sitting beside a small stream, the old man already chanting his death song.

Turn to page 155

Your muscles begin to relax as soon as you get moving again. It feels good to move more freely. Together you head for the rocky hill that is now only a dark hump against the sky. It seems very strange to be free, as if the past weeks were a bad dream. You cannot believe it, but there is no Comanche war cry from behind—maybe you have truly escaped.

This joy is short-lived, however. As you approach the rocky hill, the grass begins to thin out and suddenly there is no cover at all. You run on, certain that no one can follow your tracks on this stony ground, until you hear the sound of horses.

"Joey," you scream. "They're ahead of us."

Four mounted warriors, two with lances and two with bows, come thundering out from behind some boulders. Before you know it, they are upon you. The only sound is the horses' hooves and the zing of an arrow. Joey falls, an arrow through his throat. You do not have to look twice to know he is dead. Pulling out Buffalo Tail's knife, you wrap the buffalo robe around your arm like a shield. Quickly you ward off one arrow, then another. You slash out at a warrior's leg. It is Hiding Rabbit. He swings out of the saddle and faces you, lance in hand. The memory of your embarrassment at his hands rises up in your mind and you scream out in the cold night as you rush him. The thrust of the lance is so quick that you barely see it. Suddenly you are pinned to the ground. The stars swirl and then fade away entirely.

End

Spring is just as evident north of the slaughter as it was before, but much of the joy has gone out of it. After weeks of travel, you finally arrive at the beautiful river the Tejanos call Colorado. The days have grown warm, and the water is calm and inviting. It has been months since you bathed, and everyone wants to wash the smell of death from themselves and their clothes. Spring Flower calls for you to join her. She pulls her dress off and waits naked beside the river. "Come," she calls, before plunging in. You've never taken your clothes off in front of anyone before, but it seems the thing to do. Hiding Rabbit watches, a little too appreciatively, you think, as you join Spring Flower. Then he too strips and wades into the water.

Soon, the three of you are splashing and shouting and, little by little, you become used to the fact that no one cares that you are naked. It feels good to be clean at last.

The band camps along the Colorado throughout the summer. The Nermernuh rarely eat fish, but there are plenty of deer and antelope for Hiding Rabbit to hunt, and the snares he sets out nearly always produce a breakfast of rabbit or raccoon or opossum. The older men—Buffalo

Tail, He Who Spits, Morning Wind, and Dancing Moon—spend their days scouting and hunting, making arrows, cutting and trimming and drying new tepee poles, and talking. Coyote Eyes and Bee Woman tan deer hides, dry meats, make pemmican, and cook constantly. You and Spring Flower spend a lot of time gathering buffalo chips, firewood, herbs, and berries, looking for the few good nuts still on the ground, and talking.

Spring Flower is eager to learn all about the life of the whites but thinks that the life you describe sounds strange. "Why put seeds in the ground and wait for them to grow," she asks, "when there is food all around you?" You tell her about books, but she cannot understand why reading is important or even interesting. You tell her about cities, but the idea of a house that cannot move seems ridiculous to her. You laugh a lot.

You talk about Hiding Rabbit too. Spring Flower says he will tie horses outside your tent someday—meaning that he will ask you to marry him. Since Spring Flower is his first cousin, he cannot marry her, and you *have* noticed that he leaves a lot of little gifts—flowers, pretty stones, and shells—on your sleeping robe. You are thirteen. Your May birthday came and went without your even thinking about it. You tell Spring Flower that Hiding Rabbit is not the only brave in the world. You tell yourself that you are a long way from being ready to marry anyone.

All that summer, the men talk about the buffalo. It is difficult for them to imagine that all of the millions of buffalo on the plains have been killed, so they decide that the herds must simply be further north. As pleasant as life is along the Colorado in the summer, it will be hard to get by in the winter without a good supply of buffalo meat, new robes, and new hides for tepees. In the heat of early September, you prepare to move north, leaving Pehnahterkuh country.

Turn to page 123

Though you are sad to leave your adopted family, you choose to marry Hiding Rabbit and go north. There is no ceremony. You simply move your things into Hiding Rabbit's tepee and it is done. You are now Hiding Rabbit's woman. You are delighted.

A few days later, the trek north to the Canadian River begins. Spring Flower and Tall Feather decide to join you, so the journey is quite pleasant. It takes two weeks to cross these flat plains, and the closer you come to the meeting site, the more people join you. Nermernuh of all bands, as well as Kiowas, all travel north, talking of nothing but Ishatai's medicine and of the battles of the great Nermernuh Antelope chief, Quanah. At last you will get to see the son of Cynthia Ann.

The valley of the Canadian River is filled with tepees. Hundreds of tepees. You remember your first sight of Buffalo Tail's village and how it was not at all like what you had seen in—what was it called? —in a newspaper. (You seem to be forgetting more and more English words recently.) This encampment is like that picture. There are huge fires burning and plenty of meat roasting and lots and lots of warriors wearing lots of feathers. Hanging on the tepees are the spears and shields of

some of the greatest warriors who ever rode the plains—Quanah of the Antelopes, the Kiowa chiefs Lone Wolf and Woman's Heart, the Cheyenne leaders White Shield and Stone Calf.

In the center of the encampment, a buffalo is raised upon a tall pole, and around it the people are gathered, listening to the orators and waiting for the great dance to begin. Two matters have been settled already. Quanah is the war chief over all the others, and the first whites to feel the wrath of the tribes will be the cursed buffalo hunters whose greed for robes is starving all the nations of the plains.

Once the dancing begins, it continues nonstop for three days. The drumbeat never stops, and the ground itself seems to echo the thousands of dancing feet. It is as if the heart of the world is beating in sympathy with the song of her children, and a sense of destiny settles over all present. Ishatai goes about constantly preaching to the people that all the Indian nations will follow your example, that they will unite and flood the land with the blood of the white men. It is violent talk, and glorious.

You have been married 21 days when the delirious braves take the warpath south, confident that they are invulnera-

ble to the bullets of the hide-hunters'
rifles. Spring Flower and you scream en-
couragement as Hiding Rabbit and Tall
Feather ride by and are enveloped in the
cloud of dust raised by more than a thousand warriors.

. . .

Hiding Rabbit and Tall Feather never
returned. The horde of warriors broke
upon the tiny fort of Adobe Walls like a
great wave. But like a rock on the shore
of some faraway ocean, the fort stood
firm. There were only 28 hunters in the
fort, but they were well armed and keen
eyed. The warriors, believing in Ishatai's
medicine, took incredible risks, riding
openly into the gunfire. Hundreds died
within minutes. Their faith destroyed, the
largest Indian army in history rapidly fell
to pieces.

Each tribe blamed the other as old quar-
rels were renewed. Ishatai blamed the
Cheyennes. One of their warriors had
killed a skunk, he claimed, thus breaking
his magic. Everyone blamed Ishatai.

All the tribes, all the bands, were angry.
Primed for a great war, they began raiding
every white town, farm, and ranch on the

plains. The white soldiers and the Rangers responded by waging a bloody campaign against all the tribes of the plains.

It is a full month before you rejoin Buffalo Tail on the Red River. By then, news arrives of yet another disaster. The white soldiers surprised Quanah's large encampment of Nermernuh in Palo Duro canyon. As if slaughtering the buffalo were not enough, these soldiers killed horses—thousands of fine Comanche horses. Hundreds of tepees were burned and many warriors killed as they fought long and hard to allow the women and

children time to climb the walls of the canyon and escape. Without horses, without food or shelter, most of the survivors take the road to Oklahoma.

Buffalo Tail has you break camp one morning. You travel east into the rising sun, toward Oklahoma.

"Oklahoma is good country," says Buffalo Tail, "but it has always been home to the Kotsoteka. We will visit them, but remember, the home of the Pehnahterkuh is no more. We will pass away as surely as the buffalo."

"Not so surely," you think. In your belly there is the tiny kicking of a baby Pehnahterkuh, the child of Hiding Rabbit. To Buffalo Tail, you say, "We are not buffalo. We are Nermernuh."

End

FURTHER READING

Many books have been written on the Plains Indians in general and on the Comanches in particular, but these two substantial works on the Comanches have proven consistently accurate and insightful.

Comanches: The Destruction of a People, by T. R. Fehrenbach (Knopf, 1974).

The Comanches: Lords of the South Plains, by Ernest Wallace and E. Adamson Hoebel (University of Oklahoma Press, 1952).

Interesting capture narratives are contained in:

The Last Captive, by A. C. Greene (Encino Press, Austin, 1972).

The Boy Captives, by Clinton Smith (with J. Marvin Hunter, n.d.)

The best work of fiction about a Comanche capture is:

A Woman of the People, by Benjamin Capps (Duell, Sloan and Pearce, 1966, republished by the University of New Mexico Press, 1985).

As always, an exceptionally useful tool in studying all periods of Texas history is:

A Historical Atlas of Texas, by William C. Pool, maps by Edward Triggs and Lance Wren (Encino Press, Austin, 1975).